Day W
Pea

Vertebrate Graphics

Design and production by Vertebrate Graphics Ltd, Sheffield
www.**v-graphics**.co.uk

Day Walks in the PeakDistrict

Norman Taylor & Barry Pope

Circular routes of 8 to 12 miles ranging from
high moorland outings to walks
in the limestone dales

Day Walks in the PeakDistrict

ISBN 0-9548131-3-8

Cover photo: Andy Heading

Photography by Andy Heading. Additional photography by Barry Pope, Jon Barton, Simon Richardson and Grainne Coakley

Design by Nathan Ryder – Vertebrate Graphics Ltd
Production by Oliver Jackson – Vertebrate Graphics Ltd
Map illustrations by Vertebrate Graphics Ltd

Vertebrate Graphics

www.v-graphics.co.uk

Contents

KEY TO THE MAP SYMBOLS

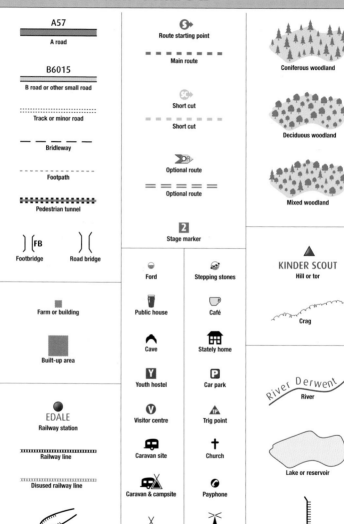

A57
A road

B6015
B road or other small road

Track or minor road

Bridleway

Footpath

Pedestrian tunnel

FB
Footbridge   Road bridge

Farm or building

Built-up area

EDALE
Railway station

Railway line

Disused railway line

Railway tunnel

Route starting point

Main route

Short cut

Short cut

Optional route

Optional route

2
Stage marker

Ford

Public house

Cave

Youth hostel

Visitor centre

Caravan site

Caravan & campsite

Campsite

Stepping stones

Café

Stately home

Car park

Trig point

Church

Payphone

Aerial or mast

Coniferous woodland

Deciduous woodland

Mixed woodland

KINDER SCOUT
Hill or tor

Crag

River Derwent
River

Lake or reservoir

Dam

Introduction

The walks described in this guide all fall within the Peak District National Park. They are evenly spread throughout the area, and reflect the great variety of landscape, flora, fauna and human settlement within the national park boundary.

The geology of the Peak has resulted in the formation of two distinct types of landscape, one defined as the Dark Peak, the other the White Peak. The moors and craggy edges in the north and to the east and west of the central area were shaped by underlying layers of sandstone of a hard, gritty consistency. This rock, known as millstone grit because it was used to make high quality millstones, becomes dark on exposure to the elements. This area is the Dark Peak.

Beneath the sandstone is a thick layer of carboniferous limestone. Where the sandstones have disappeared through erosion in the central and southern Peak, this grey-white rock has shaped the landscape. It is an area of rolling upland with occasional outcrops and deep, crag-lined limestone gorges, the part of the Peak District known as the White Peak.

Each year millions of people are drawn to the Peak District to see the sights, to climb its crags, to ride bikes along its bridleways and byways, and to explore the area on foot. If you come into the last category, we hope this guide helps you sample and enjoy the diversity of this beautiful countryside.

So, take your pick, explore, enjoy, tell your friends. We aim to please, so if you find anything wrong with this guide why not contact us at: **www.v-graphics.co.uk**

Norman Taylor & Barry Pope

Acknowledgments

The authors would like to thank the following people for their help in various ways:

Gess Boothby and Wendy Brown, Ian (Hovis) and Jacqui Brown for sterling work checking out route descriptions and highlighting any need for amendment; Dave Jepson for constructive suggestions for walks; Dave Pandya, Paul Dolling and Sarah Deakin, all of Foothills, for their willingness to be guinea pigs in testing some of the routes; Maureen Pope for acting as courier; Matt and Sam Taylor for their technical assistance with the PC; and my wife, Sue, for her encouragement and support.

About the walks

All the walks are 'day' walks in the sense that they take 5 to 6 hours to complete at an unhurried pace. They fall into three broad categories of terrain: *walks on the high moors*; *walks on lower lying hills, tors and edges*; and *walks in limestone country*.

The **summary** for each route describes the specific terrain involved, the amount of ascent, and the level of navigation skills required. We strongly recommend that you study this and the **route description** carefully before undertaking a walk.

Walk times

The time given for each walk is on the generous side. It is based on a pace of around 4 kilometres per hour/2½ miles per hour with time allowed for ascent, difficulty of terrain and stops for refreshment.

Navigation

For most walks in this guide, following the route description in combination with the route map provided, should be sufficient. However, we recommend that you carry with you the appropriate *Ordnance Survey Explorer®* series map as a back up. These are shown for each walk. The Peak District is covered by two maps in the 1:25000 series:

Ordnance Survey Explorer® OL1 (1:25,000) The Dark Peak
Ordnance Survey Explorer® OL24 (1:25,000) The White Peak

For the moorland walks a reasonable level of map reading ability and competence in the use of a compass is strongly advised. If you possess a GPS (Global Positioning System) this can be a useful navigational aid in locating your position. However, it is not a remedy for poor navigational skills.

Footpaths and rights of way

All the walks in this guide follow public rights of way or other routes with public access, including 'permitted' or 'concession' footpaths.

Safety

It is strongly advised that appropriate footwear is used – walking boots designed to provide stability and security on uneven and slippery terrain. A waterproof, windproof jacket is essential and waterproof overtrousers or trousers are strongly recommended. Sufficient insulating clothing should also be worn or carried, that is appropriate to the type of walk planned and the time of year.

Trekking poles are a definite asset since they provide greater stability and security on steep ground or slippery footpaths, thereby lessening the chances of an accident resulting from difficult terrain.

On the moorland walks emergency rations should be carried in the event of the weather causing problems or an unplanned night out! A mobile phone is an obvious asset in the event of accident – provided you can get a signal!

Mountain Rescue

In case of accident or similar need requiring mountain rescue assistance, dial 999 and ask for **POLICE – MOUNTAIN RESCUE**. Be prepared to give a 6-figure grid reference of your position in the case of a moorland location.

The Countryside Code

- **Be safe – plan ahead**
- **Leave gates and property as you find them**
- **Protect plants and animals, and take your litter home**
- **Keep dogs under close control**
- **Consider other people**

Be safe – plan ahead
Even when going out locally, it's best to get the latest information about where and when you can go; for example, your rights to go onto some areas of open land may be restricted while work is carried out, for safety reasons or during breeding seasons. Follow advice and local signs, and be prepared for the unexpected.
- Refer to up-to-date maps or guidebooks.
- You're responsible for your own safety and for others in your care, so be prepared for changes in weather and other events.
- There are many organisations offering specific advice on equipment and safety, or contact visitor information centres and libraries for a list of outdoor recreation groups.
- Check weather forecasts before you leave, and don't be afraid to turn back.
- Part of the appeal of the countryside is that you can get away from it all. You may not see anyone for hours and there are many places without clear mobile phone signals, so let someone else know where you're going and when you expect to return.

Leave gates and property as you find them
Please respect the working life of the countryside, as our actions can affect people's livelihoods, our heritage, and the safety and welfare of animals and ourselves.
- A farmer will normally leave a gate closed to keep livestock in, but may sometimes leave it open so they can reach food and water. Leave gates as you find them or follow instructions on signs; if walking in a group, make sure the last person knows how to leave the gates.
- In fields where crops are growing, follow the paths wherever possible.
- Follow paths across land that has crops growing on it, wherever possible.
- Use gates and stiles wherever possible – climbing over walls, hedges and fences can damage them and increase the risk of farm animals escaping.
- Our heritage belongs to all of us – be careful not to disturb ruins and historic sites.

- Leave machinery and livestock alone – don't interfere with animals even if you think they're in distress. Try to alert the farmer instead.

Protect plants and animals, and take your litter home
We have a responsibility to protect our countryside now and for future generations, so make sure you don't harm animals, birds, plants or trees.

- Litter and leftover food doesn't just spoil the beauty of the countryside, it can be dangerous to wildlife and farm animals and can spread disease – so take your litter home with you. Dropping litter and dumping rubbish are criminal offences.
- Discover the beauty of the natural environment and take special care not to damage, destroy or remove features such as rocks, plants and trees. They provide homes and food for wildlife, and add to everybody's enjoyment of the countryside.
- Wild animals and farm animals can behave unpredictably if you get too close, especially if they're with their young – so give them plenty of space.
- Fires can be as devastating to wildlife and habitats as they are to people and property – so be careful not to drop a match or smouldering cigarette at any time of the year. Sometimes, controlled fires are used to manage vegetation, particularly on heaths and moors between October and early April, so please check that a fire is not supervised before calling 999.

Keep dogs under close control
The countryside is a great place to exercise dogs, but it is owners' duty to make sure their dog is not a danger or nuisance to farm animals, wildlife or other people.

- By law, you must control your dog so that it does not disturb or scare farm animals or wildlife. You must keep your dog on a short lead on most areas of open country and common land between 1 March and 31 July, and at all times near farm animals.
- You do not have to put your dog on a lead on public paths as long as it is under close control. But as a general rule, keep your dog on a lead if you cannot rely on its obedience. By law, farmers are entitled to destroy a dog that injures or worries their animals.
- If a farm animal chases you and your dog, it is safer to let your dog off the lead – don't risk getting hurt by trying to protect it.
- Take particular care that your dog doesn't scare sheep and lambs or wander where it might disturb birds that nest on the ground and other wildlife – eggs and young will soon die without protection from their parents.

- Everyone knows how unpleasant dog mess is and it can cause infections – so always clean up after your dog and get rid of the mess responsibly. Also make sure your dog is wormed regularly.

- **Consider other people**
  Showing consideration and respect for other people makes the countryside a pleasant environment for everyone – at home, at work and at leisure.
  - Busy traffic on small country roads can be unpleasant and dangerous to local people, visitors and wildlife – so slow down and, where possible, leave your vehicle at home, consider sharing lifts and use alternatives such as public transport or cycling. For public transport information, phone Traveline on 0870 608 2608.
  - Respect the needs of local people – for example, don't block gateways, driveways or other entry points with your vehicle.
  - By law, cyclists must give way to walkers and horse riders on bridleways.
  - Keep out of the way when farm animals are being gathered or moved and follow directions from the farmer.
  - Support the rural economy – for example, buy your supplies from local shops.

How to use this book

This book should provide you with all of the information that you need for an enjoyable, trouble free and successful walk. The following tips should also be of help:

1. We strongly recommend that you invest in the maps listed above on page viii. These are essential even if you are familiar with the area – you may need to cut short the walk or take an alternative route.
2. Choose your route. Consider the time you have available and the abilities/level of experience of all of members your party – then read the safety section of this guide.
3. We recommend that you study the route description carefully before setting off. Cross-reference this to your OS map so that you've got a good sense of general orientation in case you need an escape route. Make sure that you are familiar with the symbols used on the maps.
4. *Get out there and get walking.*

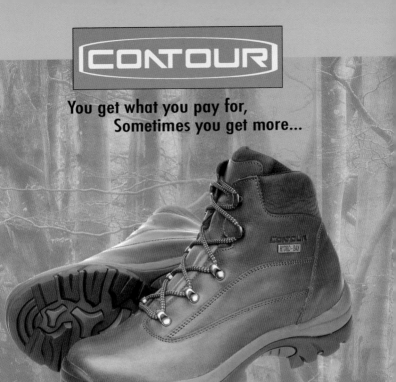

CONTOUR

You get what you pay for, Sometimes you get more...

Nevada

Standard equipment:
Comfort, Performance, Waterproof Guarantee.
Far from standard value.

Maps, Descriptions, Distances

While every effort has been made to maintain accuracy within the maps and descriptions in this guide, we have had to process a vast amount of information and we are unable to guarantee that every single detail is correct.

Please exercise caution if a direction appears at odds with the route on the map. If in doubt, a comparison between the route, the description and a quick cross-reference to your OS map (along with a bit of common sense) should help ensure that you're on the right track. Note that distances have been measured off the map, and map distances rarely coincide 100% with distances on the ground.

Please treat stated distances as a guideline only.

Km/mile conversion chart

Metric — Imperial

1 millimetre [mm]		0.03937 in
1 centimetre [cm]	10 mm	0.3937 in
1 metre [m]	100 cm	1.0936 yd
1 kilometre [km]	1000 m	0.6214 mile

Imperial — Metric

1 inch [in]		2.54 cm
1 foot [ft]	12 in	0.3048 m
1 yard [yd]	3 ft	0.9144 m
1 mile	1760 yd	1.6093 km

Thanks to:

WHO SAYS YOU CAN'T HAVE EVERYTHING?

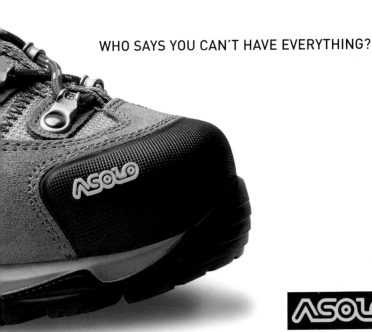

Good looks, intelligence *and* charm. The Energy Series from ASOLO really does give you the very best of all possible worlds. First, you've got the tough water-resistant upper plus a GORE-TEX®inner lining. Second, the most advanced footbed available anywhere. ASOLO's own DUO ASOFLEX® technology unifies a shock-absorbing footbed with a stiffer anti-torsion layer beneath. Add a PU midsole and bi-density outer sole unit, as well as some eye catching styling, and the Energy Series becomes a very desirable catch. But then they *are* Italian.

DUO ASOFLEX

Comfort and rigidity combined

Anti-torsion System

Bi-density Sole Unit

For more details contact Asolo on **01539 740 840** mail **asolo@lowealpine.co.uk** or visit **www.asolo.com**

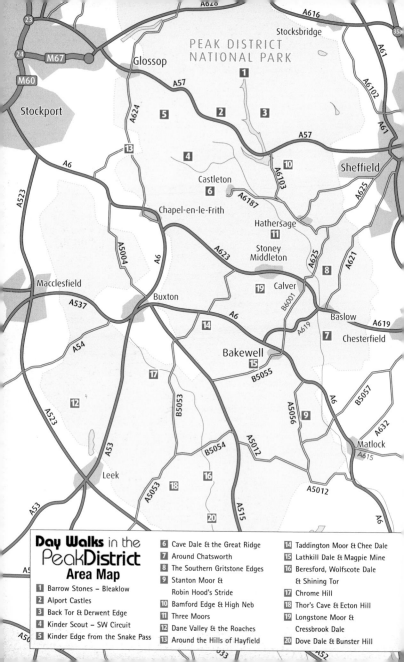

ON THE KINDER PLATEAU   PHOTO: ANDI HEADING

The High Moors

The walks in this category are located in the northern part of the Peak District. This is an area of bleak yet beckoning heather-clad moors, the habitat of red grouse, curlew and golden plover. It has remote crags, impressive deeply cut valleys, down which flow tumbling mountain streams with waterfalls and inviting pools. It is also a land of man-made forests and reservoirs that, if anything, enhance the beauty of this upland landscape.

www.rab.uk.com

A628 Woodhead Pass

BLEAKLOW

B6105

Glossop

← MANCHESTER

A57 Snake Pass

Alport Castle

5 Kinder Edge from
the Snake Pass

A624

KINDER SCOUT

Hayfield

A6015

4 Kinder Scout –
South West Circuit Edale

MAM T

A61

Stocksbridge

Barrowstones to Bleaklow

Bolsterstone

Ewden
Village

MARGERY HILL

Howden
Reservoir

BACK TOR SUMMIT

3 Back Tor &
Derwent Edge

High
Bradfield

Low
Bradfield

Derwent
Reservoir

Derwent Edge

Dungworth

SHEFFIELD ▶

Ladybower
Reservoir

A6013

HIGH NEB

LL

Hope

Bamford

**The High Moors
Area Map**

stleton

Barrow Stones – Bleaklow   15km/9.4 miles

A walk in wild moorland, to a remote corner of Bleaklow and the source of the River Derwent.

King's Tree – Black Dike – Round Hill – Barrow Stones – Humber Knolls – Slippery Stones – King's Tree

Start

King's Tree, Upper Derwent Valley. Cars and parking only permitted on weekdays. Access to King's Tree by bus from Fairholmes car park at weekends and Bank Holidays. Grid Reference 168 939

The Walk

Our route follows a steep forest track, that leads us from the starting point, up to open ground on a broad ridge. An easy trod gradually ascends within or alongside a dyke. The route crosses a track coming up from the *Westend Valley*. The ground is usually wet underfoot until it steepens and the path climbs *Round Hill*, where a windbreak of stones is well placed.

The last part of the climb, still straightforward, continues up to *Barrow Stones*.

This remote spot boasts some magnificent panoramas, highlighted by distant landmarks. From *Barrow Stones*, a diversion to the rocky promontory at *Grinah Stones* is well worth the extra kilometre or so it adds to the route.

The route leads past fascinating, wildly varied, weather-sculpted blocks of gritstone. 800m of pathless descent lead us to the infant *Derwent*, which is but a meandering stream at this point. A trod then leads to a footpath that descends alongside the maturing stream as it drops over little waterfalls, forming pools that are tempting on a hot day. The path is usually boggy in parts and a step on a steep bank is awkward underfoot. Our walk finishes along a track that leads us back, via *Slippery Stones*, to **King's Tree**.

BARROW STONES – BLEAKLOW   THE HIGH MOORS

DISTANCE: 15KM/9.4 MILES

START: GRID REFERENCE 168 939

MAP OS: *OS EXPLORER®* OL1, DARK PEAK, 1:25000

NAVIGATION: PROFICIENCY IN MAP-READING AND COMPASS SKILLS NEEDED

TOTAL ASCENT: 430 METRES/1420 FEET

TIME: ALLOW 5–5½ HOURS

REFRESHMENTS: NONE ON ROUTE

ROCK CLIMBER AT THE GRINAH STONES PHOTO: JON BARTON

PHOTO: ANDY HEADING

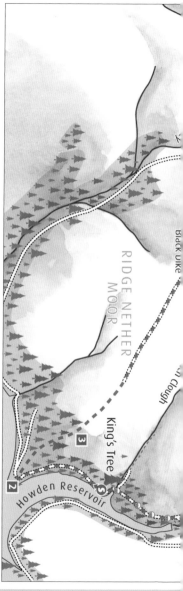

RIDGE NETHER MOOR

Black Dike

n Clough

King's Tree

2

3

Howden Reservoir

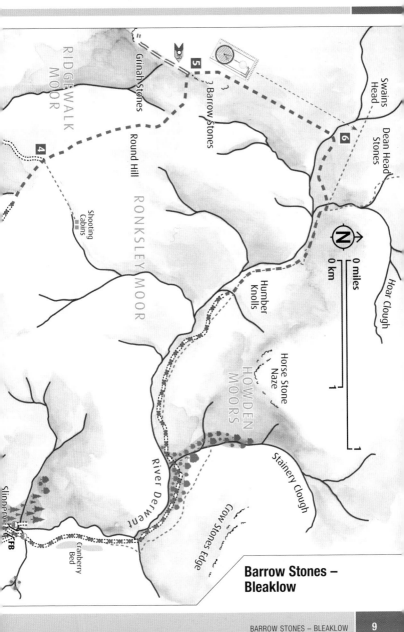

**Barrow Stones –
Bleaklow**

Directions – Barrow Stones to Bleaklow

➏ From **King's Tree** walk back along the road for 700m to the prominent right-hand bend.

2 Turn up the track on the **right** and follow this up steeply to a gate at the top of the wood.

3 **Bear half left** across the moorland meadow. The path soon becomes more obvious as it ascends parallel to a broken wall. Keep **straight on** as the path enters the dike. Follow the dike. At one point there is a **rightward** kink, after which it is better to follow the trod on its left side. Eventually a line of posts leads to the vehicle turning point on the track from the *Westend Valley*.

4 Either **turn right** on the paved path, then **turn left** in 50m, or walk **north** on a footpath, passing pools to join the latter further on. After a wet section, the path steepens as it **bears right** and climbs to a windbreak on *Round Hill* and **bears left** up to *Barrow Stones*. *

> *** ▶OR▶** To visit *Grinah Stones*, see **Optional Route** below.

5 A choice of trods leads **right** to more outlying stones. At the northern edge of the rocks, descend to a newly constructed fence. The stile is out of sight, just to the right. Cross this, walk **left** to the point where you met the fence. From here, walking on a bearing of **30° magnetic**, use a combination of trods, groughs and a grass slope to descend. After the angle eases, keep on the right of a shallow valley to avoid wet areas. Continue to the stream, which is narrow and easy to step across hereabouts.

▶▶OptionalRoute▶

For *Grinah Stones* follow the trod to the **left** for 600m, then retrace your steps.

6 **Bear right**, follow sheep trods through heather above and parallel to the stream to begin with, then **bear left** after 500m to join the main footpath descending from *Swain's Head* to *Hoar Clough*. Follow the path down the valley, with one awkward step by the river's edge, avoidable by a higher level trod through bracken. The path becomes a track after a short ascent from the stream. Follow the track back to the packhorse bridge at *Slippery Stones*. Cross it and keep **straight on** to *King's Tree*.

FROZEN RUSHES **PHOTO:** *BARRY POPE*

Alport Castles

This varied walk takes in lakeside, forest and open moor, and has the remarkable landslip feature known as Alport Castles as its focal point.

Fairholmes – Bridgend – Lockerbrook Heights – Alport Castles – Alport –
Roman road – Rowlee Bridge – Lockerbrook Heights – Fairholmes

Start
Fairholmes car park,
Upper Derwent Valley
Grid Reference 173 893

The Walk
The route starts, following a path that takes us through woods alongside *Ladybower* for a kilometre. It joins an ancient bridleway that leads up through forest to high, open pastures on a broad ridge. We have uninterrupted views from the ridge, across to *Kinder Scout*, the *Great Ridge* and the *Vale of Edale*.

Our route gradually ascends the broad ridge for 4km, to a sensational viewpoint above the naturally formed, but quarry-like, craggy landscape of the landslip known as **Alport Castles**. Some of the topographical features within this landslip bear some resemblance to castle ruins.

From this airy spot above the deep, narrow valley of *Alport Dale* the route descends to the isolated hamlet of **Alport**. To avoid any road walking, the route then follows a track that leads to the *A57*, crossing the road and the *River Ashop*. It continues along a short section of the Roman road before re-crossing the river and the road. A track then leads us uphill to **Lockerbrook**.

Our route ends with a descent along a forest path that heads directly back to **Fairholmes**.

ALPORT CASTLES
THE HIGH MOORS

DISTANCE: 15.3KM/9.5 MILES
START: GRID REFERENCE 173 893
MAP OS: *OS EXPLORER* OL1, DARK PEAK, 1:25000
NAVIGATION: STRAIGHTFORWARD ON CLEAR PATHS AND TRACKS.

TOTAL ASCENT: 589 METRES/1933 FEET
TIME: ALLOW 5–5½ HOURS
REFRESHMENTS: NONE ON ROUTE

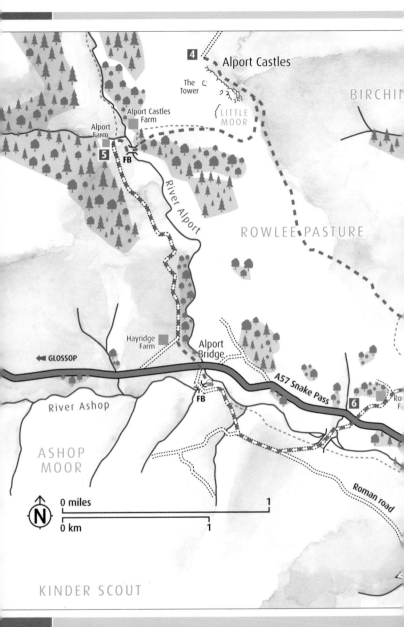

4 Alport Castles

The
Tower

BIRCHIN

LITTLE
MOOR

Alport Castles
Farm

Alport
Farm

5

FB

River Alport

ROWLEE PASTURE

Hayridge
Farm

Alport
Bridge

◀◀ GLOSSOP

A57 Snake Pass

6

Ro
F

FB

River Ashop

ASHOP
MOOR

Roman road

0 miles   1

Ⓝ

0 km   1

KINDER SCOUT

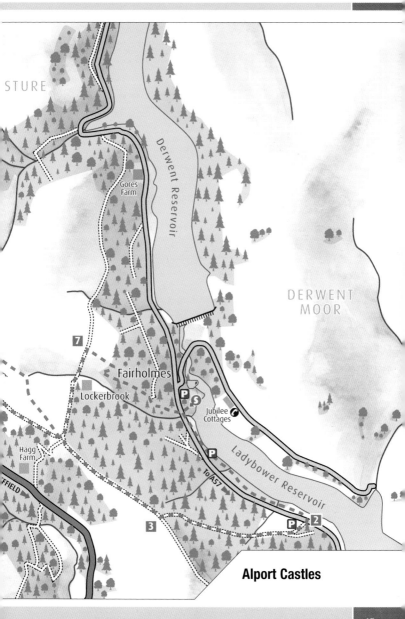

Alport Castles

Directions – Alport Castles

⑤► From the car park walk back to the road, **turn left** and continue to *Overlook* car park. **Bear left** along a path between the road and the reservoir to *Bridgend* car park (about a kilometre).

2 Take the bridleway track that leads up through the forest from the edge of the car park.

3 On emerging on a ridge at the forest edge, **turn right** and follow the path with the forest on the right to where it joins a gravel track after a stile or gate at a right-hand bend. **Cross** the track and continue **straight ahead** uphill to a ladder stile. Keep **straight on**. The path becomes paved for about 1.5km, then reverts to a spongy, wet footpath as it approaches **Alport Castles**. Continue as far as the remains of a wall that lies, oddly, at right angles to to the cliff edge (viewpoint).

4 Retrace your steps for 500m, then **bear right** along a footpath descending into *Alport Dale*. This descends quite steeply to a footbridge over the *River Alport*. **Bear right** after the bridge and continue up to *Alport*.

5 Follow the track down to the *A57*, **bearing downhill to the left** along a footpath just before reaching the farm. This leads to *Alport Bridge*. Cross the road and go down the track opposite via a gate to cross the *River Ashop* by a footbridge. Stay on the track, which climbs to a gate and junction with another track (Roman road). **Turn left**, follow the Roman road for 300m, then take a **left fork** downhill. This leads back across the river and goes up to the *A57*.

6 Cross the road and continue uphill past *Rowlee Farm* along another track. Follow it to a fork at a left-hand bend, then **bear left** down to *Lockerbrook Outdoor Centre*. Carry on along the track for a further 250m.

7 Cross the stile on the right and follow the waymarked path into woodland and downhill to **Fairholmes** via a short section on a gravel track.

OVER BELLHAGG WOOD **PHOTO:** BARRY POPE

Back Tor & Derwent Edge 17km/10.6 miles

A varied walk on clear footpaths, with stunning valley and upland scenery.

Fairholmes (Upper Derwent) – Abbey Brook – Lost Lad – Back Tor – Whinstone Lee Tor – Ladybower Reservoir – Fairholmes

Start

Fairholmes car park below the Derwent Dam in the Upper Derwent Valley.
Grid Reference 173 893

The Walk

This route follows track along the tree-lined shore of the *Derwent Reservoir*, nearly as far as *Howden Dam*. A short, steep pull leads to easier ground, where a gradually ascending footpath takes us through the deep, winding valley of *Abbey Brook*. This closes in to form an impressive steep-sided gorge in its upper reaches, with spectacular landslip features.

At this point, our route escapes from the confines of the gorge along a path that leads out on to open moorland and onward to the cairn on the rounded hill at *Lost Lad*.

A short stretch along a paved footpath affords us an easy route to **Back Tor**, a gritstone outcrop on **Derwent Edge** and the highest point on the walk. This is a place to savour the panorama that extends in all directions. A descending path now takes our route south along *Derwent Edge*. Along the way, it passes other tors and the fascinating weathered rock features known as the *Cakes of Bread*, the *Salt Cellar* and the *Coach and Horses* – all aptly named.

All too soon, it is time to descend by means of a bridleway to the banks of *Ladybower Reservoir*. On the last leg, our route passes the site of the drowned village of *Derwent*.

BACK TOR & DERWENT EDGE

THE HIGH MOORS

DISTANCE: 17KM/10.6 MILES
START: GRID REFERENCE 173 893
MAP OS: *OS EXPLORER®* OL1, DARK PEAK, 1:25000

TOTAL ASCENT: 430 METRES/1400 FEET
TIME: ALLOW 5-6 HOURS
REFRESHMENTS: NONE ON ROUTE

NAVIGATION: ALTHOUGH CLEAR FOOTPATHS ARE USED THROUGHOUT, PROFICIENCY IN MAP AND COMPASS SKILLS IS RECOMMENDED.

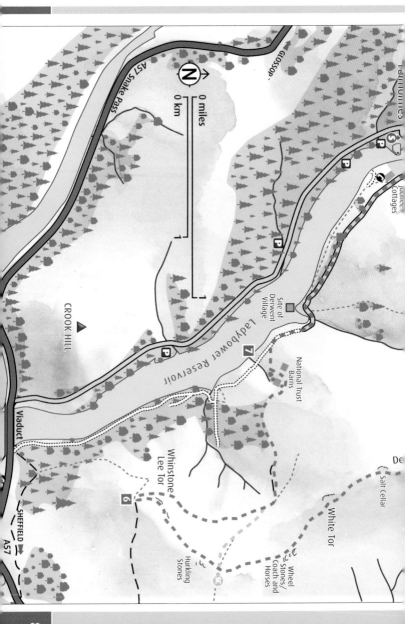

N

0 miles

0 km

A57 Snake Pass

Glossop -

Fairholmes

Jubilee Cottages

CROOK HILL

Site of Derwent Village

Ladybower Reservoir

7

National Trust Barns

Viaduct

SHEFFIELD

A57

Whinstone Lee Tor

6

Hurkling Stones

Salt Cellar

White Tor

Wheel Stones/ Coach and Horses

De

Derwent Reservoir

Howden
Reservoir

Walker's
Clough

Far Deep Clough

Abbey Brook

LOST LAD

Back Tor

Howshaw Tor

Sheepfold Clough

Cakes of Bread

**Back Tor &
Derwent Edge**

Directions – Back Tor & Derwent Edge

❺▸ Walk below the *Derwent Dam* and climb steps beside the right-hand tower to join the track on the east side of the *Derwent Reservoir*. **Turn left** and follow this for just over 2km to the *second* signposted footpath on the right (*Ewden*).

2 **Bear right** off the track and follow the path up, taking a **left fork** after the initial steep section. Continue along the gradually ascending footpath, which keeps parallel with the brook. After 2km, prominent landslips form a spectacular feature within the gorge. At the same point, *Sheepfold Clough* joins on the right.

3 Take a **right fork** and follow a footpath up the clough and out of the gorge on to open moorland. Continue to a paved footpath.

4 **Turn left** and follow this up to the cairn at *Lost Lad*, then continue for a further 0.5km to **Back Tor**.

5 **Turn right** and follow the path along **Derwent Edge** for nearly 4km, to the second footpath crossroads.*

> *❌▸ *Turning right* at the first footpath crossroads would lead to the bridleway described below in **6** and shorten the route by 1.5km.)

6 **Turn right** on the bridleway and follow it downhill. Pass through a gateway, and keep **straight on** down past *Grindle Barn* to the banks of *Ladybower*.

7 **Turn right** and follow the lane back to **Fairholmes**, passing the site of Derwent Village en route.

23

KINDER SCOUT – SOUTH WEST CIRCUIT

THE HIGH MOORS

DISTANCE: 15.8 KM / 9.7 MILES

START: GRID REFERENCE 124 853

MAP OS: OS EXPLORER OL1 DARK PEAK 1:25000

TOTAL ASCENT: 570 METRES/1870 FEET

TIME: ALLOW 6 HOURS

REFRESHMENTS: NONE ON ROUTE.
PUBS AND A CAFÉ IN EDALE

NAVIGATION: ALTHOUGH THE PATHS USED ARE CLEAR TO FOLLOW, AMBIGUITIES AND ROUTE FINDING
DIFFICULTIES COULD BE EXPERIENCED IN MISTY OR WINTRY CONDITIONS. SKILLS IN THE USE OF MAP AND
COMPASS ARE THEREFORE ADVISABLE.

THE RIVER NOE AT JACOB'S LADDER   **PHOTO:** ANDY HEADING

Kinder Scout – South West Circuit

15.6km/9.7 miles

This walk has a mountain character, using an old packhorse route in ascent. Then it follows a high-level path, to take in some incredible natural rock features and stunning scenery along the way.

Edale – Barber Booth – Upper Booth – Swine's Back – Crowden Tower – Ringing Rodger – Edale

Start

Edale Pay-and-Display car park.
Grid Reference 124 853

The Walk

From **Edale**, our route follows a path across fields to the hamlet of *Barber Booth* and on to *Upper Booth*. The Old Norse term 'booth' refers to summer pastures.

A track leads us past a wood turner's cottage, continuing to the packhorse bridge at the foot of *Jacob's Ladder*. We follow the paved footpath that heads straight up the hillside, making for the saddle at *Edale Cross*. Alternatively, the old bridlepath takes a less direct approach to gain height.

Our climb from the saddle continues a little further. The going becomes easier as we reach the high-level path that follows the edge of the summit plateau. The undulating footpath passes two rock features, shown on the map as *Noe Stool* and *Pym Chair*, then takes us into the amazing area of eroded rocks, known as the *Wool Packs*. Some of these do resemble wool packs, but some are more like giant mushrooms or chess pieces, whilst others are more animalistic in their features.

A little further on, *Crowden Tower*, a tall gritstone crag, dominates *Crowden Clough*. A stretch of paved footpath leads us to the craggy cirque of *Grindsbrook Clough* overlooking *Edale*. The path clings to the rim of the cirque, offering ever-changing views, as we progress across the tops of crags, or 'tors'. The route off the top takes us down one of the lesser-known footpaths, that takes a more gradual line than most. We follow a series of gradually descending zig-zags back to the valley bottom and on to **Edale** to end our walk.

DESCENDING TOWARDS EDALE FROM GRINDSBROOK CLOUGH
PHOTO: ANDY HEADING

PHOTO: JON BARTON

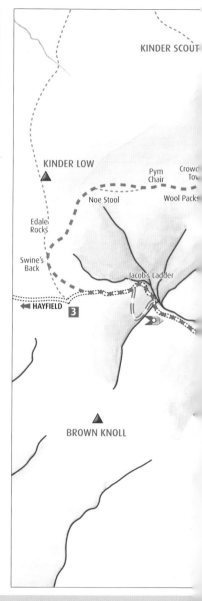

KINDER SCOUT

KINDER LOW

Pym
Chair

Crowc
Tov

Noe Stool

Wool Packs

Edale
Rocks

Swine's
Back

Jacob's Ladder

◄ HAYFIELD **3**

BROWN KNOLL

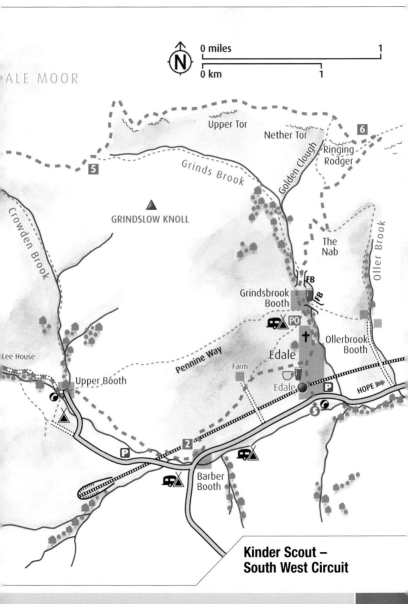

Kinder Scout –
South West Circuit

Directions – Kinder Scout – South West Circuit

➎ Leave the car park, passing the toilets, and walk up the road towards **Edale** village. At the first right-hand bend, **turn left** (fingerpost) and head for a handgate. Continue along the obvious footpath. Pass below a farm, cross a track, and **bear half left** down a field. Continue to a railway bridge, cross it and enter *Barber Booth*.

2 **Keep right** in the hamlet, passing a chapel, join a track and cross the railway again. **Turn left** and follow the obvious path across fields to the farm at *Upper Booth*, where you **turn left** to join the lane. **Turn right** and follow the lane/track to a footbridge at the foot of *Jacob's Ladder*. Use the paved footpath or take the more gradually ascending bridlepath up the hillside. Continue climbing fairly steeply, until you reach a short, level section with a resting place.

3 Take the **right fork** off the main footpath. This soon joins a path that climbs from the saddle between *Brown Knoll* and *Kinder Scout*. Continue uphill to where it levels out near the rocks of *Swine's Back*. The path climbs gently to *Noe Stool*, and continues to the rocky outcrop at the back of which is *Pym Chair*. From here the path, or rather multiplicity of paths, passes through the *Wool Packs*, The easiest of these skirts the rocks on the north side. If the weather conditions deteriorate at this point, **head due east**. Continue another 250m or so to *Crowden Tower* on the right of the footpath and overlooking the deeply incised valley of *Crowden Clough*.

4 Either descend, with difficulty, the steep gravelly path, then cross the brook. A better alternative is to **bear left** and follow a footpath that heads back into the wilderness of the plateau crossing two streams before returning to the edge footpath, having bypassed the difficult stretches. Continue along the edge footpath, later stretches of which are paved. At a fork adjacent to prominent stones **go left** along the paving stones. This leads to the top of the craggy cirque of *Grindsbrook Clough*.

5 **Turn left**. Keep to the edge footpath. This makes a 500m detour, first to the north, then south, as it crosses the top of a crag-lined gully before it can head eastwards. Continue along the obvious path, often paved, and staying close to the edge. This is much easier and less erosive than wading through peaty sections further left. The path climbs a little as it passes above *Upper Tor*, then continues across the top of

Nether Tor. 300m further on is the top of *Golden Clough*, with footpaths leading steeply downhill. Ignore these and take the higher level of two footpaths. This reaches a protected enclosure above the rocks of *Ringing Rodger.* **Bear half left** after crossing the stile to emerge in 150m at another stile.

6 Continue **left** for 100m, then take the narrow path that doubles back downhill below *Ringing Rodger* (difficult to make out until you are in line with it). Continue to a path junction, then **turn left**. Take the next rightward option to zigzag down *The Nab.* This becomes paved. Continue down to the valley bottom, **bearing left** to pick up the path that crosses the river and enters *Edale.* Keep **straight on** to reach the car park.

PHOTO: *ANDY HEADING*

PHOTO: *ANDY HEADING*

NEARING EDALE CROSS ON JACOB'S LADDER   PHOTO: *ANDY HEADING*

ICE CLIMBER ON KINDER DOWNFALL PHOTO: BARRY ROPER

Kinder Edge
from the Snake Pass

14km/8.75 miles

Craggy, steep-sided slopes, tumbling streams, remote gritstone crags and long-distance views over wild country give this route the atmosphere and character of a mountain walk.

Birchen Clough – Fair Brook – Fair Brook Naze – Kinder Edge – Ashop Head – Ashop Clough – Birchen Clough

Start

Birchen Clough lay-by
1km up the A57 from the Snake Inn.
Grid Reference 109 914

The Walk

Our route follows the footpath that leads up to the *Kinder Plateau*. It takes us through the gorge etched out by *Fair Brook*, a mountain stream with waterfalls and deep, clear pools. The path is awkward in parts, especially the last half kilometre, which climbs steeply. The best way up this section is to stay close to the stream.

The path along the rim of the plateau continues north to the promontory at *Fairbrook Naze*. There are exceptionally fine views of the deep valleys and surrounding high moors. We follow an obvious but sinuous path in a westerly direction across the top of *The Edge*. It weaves its way over and around eroded rocks and boulders, and across peaty sections. The best choice of route here is always near the rocks at the edge of the crag.

Our route eventually joins the **Pennine Way** footpath. A 3km diversion allows us to see the spectacular craggy amphitheatre of *Kinder Downfall*. The descent uses the *Snake Path*, which follows *Ashop Clough*. The stream and the path share the same course for a short section, but fortunately, this does not last for long and the path soon improves. The gorge deepens and the stream becomes a river. Our path clings to the steep valley side as it descends to the *Snake Pass* and the end of our walk.

KINDER EDGE FROM THE SNAKE PASS	THE HIGH MOORS
DISTANCE: 14KM/8.75 MILES	**TOTAL ASCENT:** 560 METRES/1835 FEET
START: GRID REFERENCE 109 914	**TIME:** ALLOW 5-6 HOURS
MAP OS: *OS EXPLORER*® OL1, DARK PEAK, 1:25000	**REFRESHMENTS:** NONE ON ROUTE
NAVIGATION: PROFICIENCY IN MAP-READING AND COMPASS SKILLS NEEDED	

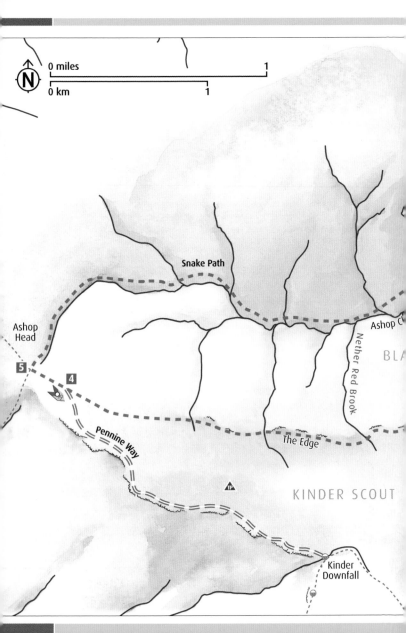

0 miles 1

0 km 1

N

Snake Path

Ashop
Head

Ashop C

BLA

Nether Red Brook

5

4

Pennine Way

The Edge

KINDER SCOUT

Kinder
Downfall

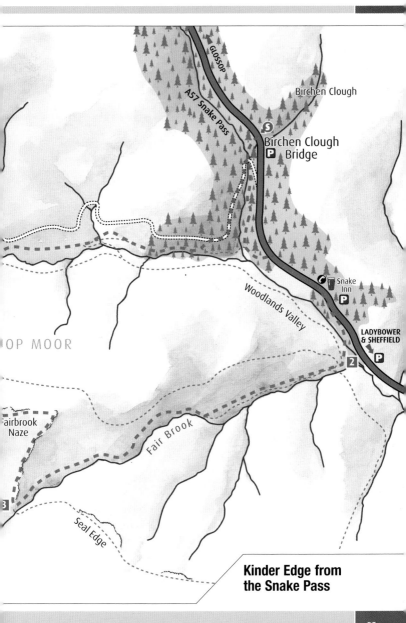

Glossop

Birchen Clough

A57 Snake Pass

Birchen Clough
Bridge

Snake
Inn

LADYBOWER
& SHEFFIELD

Woodlands Valley

OP MOOR

2

Fairbrook
Naze

Fair Brook

3

Seal Edge

**Kinder Edge from
the Snake Pass**

Directions – Kinder Edge from the Snake Pass

➔ From **Birchen Clough** cross the main road and descend steps to reach the riverside footpath, then **turn left**. Cross a track and stay on the riverside path. On passing through a gate, **bear left**. The path soon ascends to the A57. **Turn right** and follow the roadside path to the *Snake Inn*. Opposite the car park, cross a stile on the right. Continue through the wood more or less parallel to the main road, eventually **bearing right** down to cross the *River Ashop* by the footbridge.

2 Follow the path above the *River Ashop* then **bear right** into the valley of *Fair Brook*. The path climbs parallel with the brook for most of its two kilometre length to reach the plateau. The best way to tackle the last steep section is to stay on the immediate right of the stream as it tumbles over the rocks, ignoring the temptation to move to higher possibilities which would prove to be more difficult.

3 **Turn right** at the top and follow the indefinite path along the rim of the plateau to the promontory at *Fairbrook Naze*. The path now **turns west** and follows the top of *The Edge* for just over 2km, where the rim of plateau now **turns southeast**. This joins the **Pennine Way**.

OptionalRoute

If you have the time and inclination, **turn left** on the **Pennine Way** and walk for 1.5km to the *Downfall*, then retrace your steps.

4 **Turn right** to continue west along the **Pennine Way** footpath. After a steep descent on inlaid stones the path reaches a junction at *Ashop Head*.

5 **Turn right** and take the **Snake Path** down *Ashop Clough*. The first part is paved, but this does not last for long, and a wet section has to be negotiated for a short distance before the path improves. About 4km from *Ashop Head* the path enters a plantation. At a waymark post with white markings, **bear left**. This path climbs a little, then makes a gradual descent and joins a forest track. This descends to cross the *River Ashop*. **Turn left** and retrace the outward route, heading up to the right in 100m.

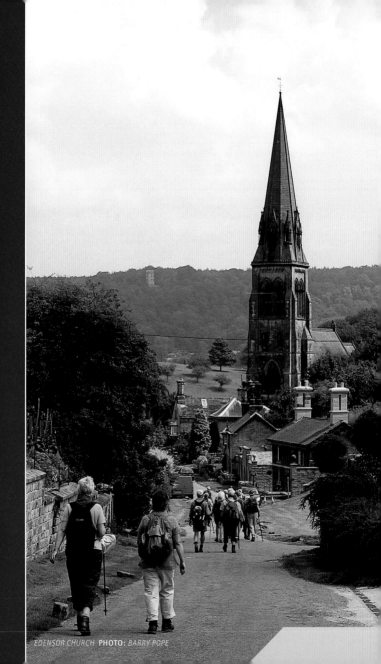

EDENSOR CHURCH **PHOTO:** *BARRY POPE*

SECTION 2

Hills, Tors & Edges

*The area in which the walks in this
category fall is located to the south of the
high moors and includes the eastern and
western borderlands of the Peak District.
Here the landscape is characterised by
broad ridges, with hilltops, gritstone tors
and escarpments with craggy edges.
This is a varied landscape of wooded
river valleys and 'cloughs', wild meadows,
pasture and scattered farmsteads, of lower
lying moors with stone circles and other
ancient relics.*

www.lowealpine.com

CORK STONE ON STANTON MOOR **PHOTO:** ANDY HEADING

Marple

Hayfield

13 Around the
Hills of Hayfield

A6015

Cave Dale & **6**
the Great Ridge

Cas

A6

Chapel-en-
le-Frith

B5470

A5004

Bollington

Buxton

A537

A53

A54

B6053

A515

Dane Valley **12**
& the Roaches

10 Bamford Edge & High Neb

SHEFFIELD

A6101

A6013

Hope

Bradwell

Hathersage

A6187

11 Three Moors

A61

8 The Southern Gritstone Edges

Baslow

A6020

A6

Chesterfield

A613

Bakewell

7 Around Chatsworth

Northwood

A632

Stanton Moor & **9** Robin Hood's Stride

Matlock

Hills, Tors & Edges Area Map

Winster

CAVE DALE ON A GREY NOVEMBER DAY   PHOTO: BARRY POPE

Cave Dale & the Great Ridge

15.2km/9.5 miles

This exhilarating walk combines riverside, a limestone gorge and a ridge with three prominent summits. On a clear day there are fine views from the ridge.

Hope – Castleton – Cave Dale – Windy Knoll – Mam Tor – Lose Hill – Hope

Start

Hope. Village car park or roadside.
Grid Reference 171 835

The Walk

Our route follows a riverside path to *Castleton*. We follow the narrow limestone gorge of **Cave Dale** that leads steeply uphill to the high pastures above the village. Level walking along tracks provides a breather before we climb to the summit of *Mam Tor*.

The route passes a cave at *Windy Knoll*. When this site was excavated by archaeologists, it yielded various prehistoric artefacts that suggest that the cave was used as a temporary shelter by nomadic Stone Age hunter-gatherers. *Mam Tor* was the site of an Iron Age hill fort and the ramparts and other earthworks are still clearly discernible. The summit is a prime viewpoint and its popularity with tourists has made it necessary to lay setts to prevent further erosion of the hillside.

Our route now descends to the ancient crossing point at *Hollins Cross* before climbing *Back Tor*. After another dip in the ridge the path climbs to *Lose Hill* summit, another splendid viewpoint. We finish by descending to **Hope** through fields.

CAVE DALE & THE GREAT RIDGE	HILLS, TORS & EDGES
DISTANCE: 15.2KM/9.5 MILES	**TOTAL ASCENT:** 580 METRES/1890 FEET
START: GRID REFERENCE 171 835	**TIME:** ALLOW 5½ HOURS
MAP OS: *OS EXPLORER*® OL1, DARK PEAK, 1:25000	**REFRESHMENTS:** NONE AFTER CASTLETON
NAVIGATION: STRAIGHTFORWARD	

MAM TOR SUMMIT PHOTO: BARRY POPE

MOUNTAIN BIKERS ON THE GREAT RIDGE PHOTO: ANDY HEADING

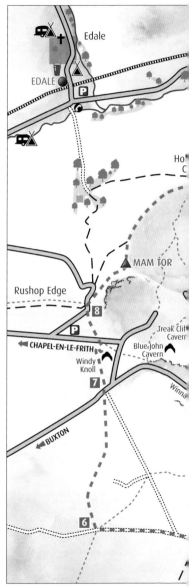

Edale

EDALE

Ho
C

▲ MAM TOR

Rushop Edge

8

P

← CHAPEL-EN-LE-FRITH

Treak Clif
Caverr

Blue John
Cavern

Windy
Knoll

7

Winna

← BUXTON

6

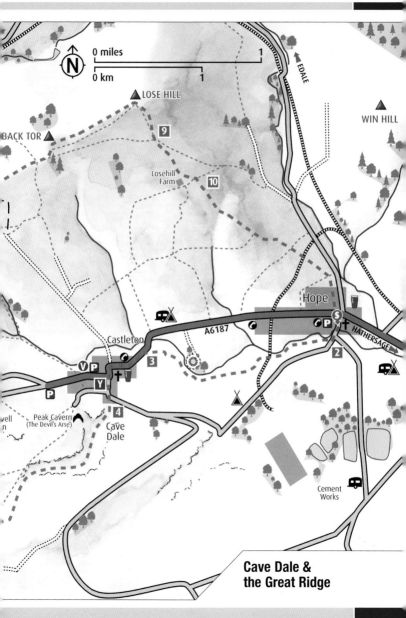

0 miles 1

0 km 1

N

▲ LOSE HILL

WIN HILL ▲

BACK TOR ▲

EDALE

9

Losehill Farm

10

Hope

A6187

HATHERSAGE

Castleton

3

2

V **P**

Y

P

Peak Cavern
(The Devil's Arse)

4

Cave Dale

vell
n

Cement Works

Cave Dale & the Great Ridge

Directions – Cave Dale and the Great Ridge

➏ Turn down the road to *Pin Dale* by the Woodroffe Arms. Continue over the bridge and up to a stile on the right.

2 Cross this and follow the riverside footpath. This leads to *Castleton*, crossing a railway track en route.

3 **Turn left** on joining the main road. Walk as far as the *Nag's Head* at the second right-angled bend. Continue up to the **left** of the hotel along *Back Street*. Carry on past the old market square and **bear left** on the minor road. In a short distance, **turn right** to enter **Cave Dale** (signposted).

4 Follow the steepening path up through the narrow gorge. **Bear right** through a bridlegate, and continue more easily through fields to arrive at a gate with stile.

5 **Turn right**, pass through another gate, then continue along the track. Keep **straight on** at the fork. Follow the track uphill for 600m to a stile on the right just before a gate.

6 Cross the stile and follow the path with a wall on the left. After two stiles, the path descends to a gate and the main road.

7 Cross the road, go through the gate opposite and keep **straight on** with a wall on the left. (*Windy Knoll* and the cave are to the right of the path.) On arriving at another road, cross it and the handgate opposite, then follow the ascending path up to a stile at *Mam Nick*.

8 **Bear right** along the paved path that climbs to the summit of *Mam Tor*. Continue along the undulating ridge via *Hollins Cross* and *Back Tor* for 3.5km to the summit of *Lose Hill*. Continue down the other side to a stile. Cross it, then take a **right fork**.

9 After crossing another stile in a few metres, **turn sharp left** to follow a path down to farm buildings.

10 Just left of the farm, cross a stile on the right, then keep **straight on** downhill, exiting the second field by a stile on the left. Continue along the obvious path. Keep a straight course to emerge opposite the *Woodroffe Arms*.

PHOTO: ANDY HEADING

THE WOODBINE CAFÉ IN HOPE   PHOTO: JON BARTON

PHOTO: ANDY HEADING

PHOTO: ANDY HEADING

CHATSWORTH HOUSE **PHOTO:** *ANDY HEADING*

Around Chatsworth

18km/11 miles

A walk through an incredible mix of man-made and natural landscape, that includes hill pastures, woodland, lakes, open moor and riverside.

Calton Lees – Calton Houses – Ballcross Farm – Edensor – Chatsworth House – Hunting Tower – Beeley Moor – Beeley – Calton Lees

Start

Calton Lees picnic area in Chatsworth Park on the B6012 1.6km south of Chatsworth House.
Grid Reference 258 685

The Walk

From the justly popular riverside pastures at **Calton Lees** in *Chatsworth Park*, a gradual climb on tracks and field paths leads us to the sheep pastures above the valley, and on to a viewpoint overlooking the hills and valleys west of *Baslow*.

Our route now descends to the estate village of *Edensor*. Designed by Joseph Paxton, the original village, sited nearer the house, was demolished and rebuilt in its present form in the 1830s. *Queen Mary's Bower* is just a short walk away. It dates from the 16th Century and may have been used by Mary Queen of Scots during her incarceration at Chatsworth in the 1570s.

The climb from the river takes us past *Chatsworth House* and the *Farmyard*, then continues steeply up the delightful wooded hillside. We visit the broken aqueduct and waterfall en route to the *Hunting Tower*, built as a summer house for Bess of Hardwick in the 16th Century. On from here, a forest track leads us round past *Emperor* and *Swiss Lakes*. Outside the park, the landscape changes abruptly to open moorland with views across the river valley.

We descend to the estate village of *Beeley*, then stroll across riverside meadows to round off a varied outing.

AROUND CHATSWORTH

HILLS, TORS & EDGES

DISTANCE: 18KM/11 MILES
START: GRID REFERENCE 258 685
MAP OS: *OS EXPLORER®* OL24, WHITE PEAK, 1:25000
NAVIGATION: STRAIGHTFORWARD

TOTAL ASCENT: 468 METRES/1537 FEET
TIME: ALLOW 5-5½ HOURS
REFRESHMENTS: TEASHOP AT EDENSOR. STABLES TEASHOP AT CHATSWORTH HOUSE. DEVONSHIRE ARMS AT BEELEY.

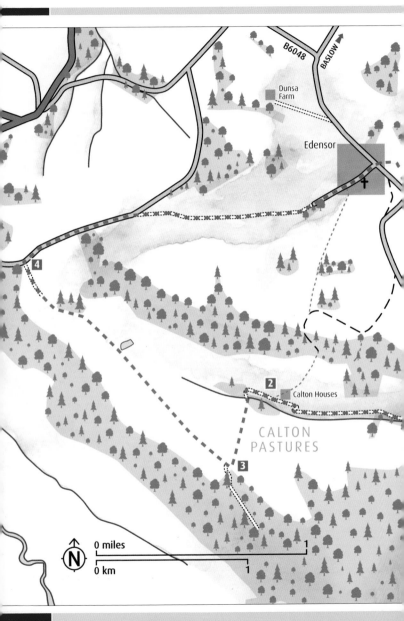

B6048

BASLOW

Dunsa
Farm

Edensor

4

2 Calton Houses

CALTON
PASTURES

3

0 miles 1

0 km 1

N

Chatsworth Park

Queen Mary's Bower

5

7 Farmyard

Hunting Tower

Emperor Lake

Chatsworth House

6

⊞ STATELY HOME

Swiss Lake

Swiss Cottage

Park Farm

8

Beeley Hilltop

9

Stone Circle

Garden Centre

B6012

River Derwent

Datley Dale

10

Beeley

Around Chatsworth

Directions – Around Chatsworth

❺➤ Follow the road that passes above the *garden centre*, then bends right into a valley. Keep **straight on** through a gate and along the track uphill to *Calton Houses*. Continue past the cottages and through a bridlegate.

2 **Turn left** and stay parallel with the wall on the left, then go **left** through a gate between woods. **Bear slightly left** and ascend the hillside – posts guide the way – to the edge of a walled plantation.

3 Instead of going through the wood, **turn right** and follow the field path as it first contours then gradually descends to the left side of a pond. Keep **straight on** and **pass just left** of a wooded knoll. A track is soon joined which leads to a lane.

4 **Turn right**. Follow the lane over the hilltop then downhill to where a track **forks right** off the lane. Follow this downhill to and through Edensor. Cross the main road, then take the gravel path opposite. This leads to a bridge. Cross it and walk up and past *Chatsworth House*. **Pass left** of *The Stables* and approach the *Farmyard* after a cattle grid.

5 Follow the tarmac lane uphill past the *Farmyard*. Take the path **bearing uphill to the left** signposted *"The Dell"*. Cross a lane and continue uphill along the path that passes beneath the broken aqueduct. Stay on the right of the tumbling stream and carry on up to the top of the waterfalls.

6 Descend the steps on the other side, then stay on the path that contours the hillside. Ignore further steps that descend to the left. Eventually, the path emerges at the *Hunting Tower*.

7 **Turn right** facing the Tower and walk along a path to a track. Follow this, ignoring any rightward options. The track winds round past *Emperor* and *Swiss Lakes* and after 2km reaches a crossroads. Go **straight across**. Stay on the track, which soon **bears left** to a gate and stile.

8 Keep **straight on** along the track for about 1.5km, to where it ends at a gate and stile. Cross the stile and **turn right** to follow the track downhill for another 1.5km to *Beeley Hilltop Farm*.

9 **Turn left** at the fingerpost/stile. **Bear right** across the farmyard and go through a gate. Keep **straight on** with a wall on the left, then maintain the same course downhill. Follow the obvious field path via stiles into *Beeley*.

10 **Turn left**, then **right** by the church. Cross the main road and go through the gate opposite. Follow the path across the field to the road bridge. After crossing this, **turn right** through a gate to walk alongside the river, then **bear left** before the ruin up to the road and the car park.

PHOTO: ANDY HEADING

The Southern Gritstone Edges

18.5km/11.5 miles

High level footpaths, continuously changing views and impressive crags characterise this walk along the Southern Gritstone Edges.

Baslow – Baslow Edge – Curbar – Froggatt – Grouse Inn – White Edge – Gardom's Edge – Chatsworth Edge – Baslow

Start

**Baslow. The walk is described from the Pay-and-Display car park.
Grid Reference 258 721**

The Walk

From **Baslow**, a track leads us uphill to *Wellington's Monument* on *Baslow Edge*. The 'Gritstone Edges' form an escarpment, two-tiered for some of its length. From these abrupt sandstone crags, so popular with climbers, the slope descends gently eastwards.

On its outward journey, our route follows paths north along the top of *Baslow*, *Curbar* and *Froggatt Edges*, then climbs slightly higher to the overlying escarpment of *White Edge*. The path along here leads us south, then continues along the top of the much less frequented *Gardom's Edge*. We also take in *Chatsworth Edge*, before finally descending through *Chatsworth Park* to finish.

The views along the way justify the popularity of these cragtop footpaths, although some sections along *White Edge* can be muddy after wet weather. A short exposed section of footpath along the top of *Chatsworth Edge* can be a problem for those that suffer from vertigo, but this can be avoided by taking a lower-level footpath.

Deer can often be sighted in *Chatsworth Park* – an added bonus on this route.

THE SOUTHERN GRITSTONE EDGES

HILLS, TORS & EDGES

DISTANCE: 18.5KM/11.5 MILES
START: GRID REFERENCE 258 721
MAP OS: *OS EXPLORER®* OL24, WHITE PEAK, 1:25000
NAVIGATION: STRAIGHTFORWARD ON WELL-USED PATHS

TOTAL ASCENT: 500 METRES/1660 FEET
TIME: ALLOW 6 HOURS
REFRESHMENTS: THE GROUSE INN AT THE HALFWAY MARK AND THE ROBIN HOOD INN 2.5KM FROM THE END.

Calver

Curbar

A619

Baslow

Eaton Hill

Bar Road

Baslow Edge

Eagle Stone

Wellington's Monument

Jubilee Rock

A619

A621

Gardom's Edge

Chatsworth Edge

Moorside Rocks

BASLOW COMMON

Robin Hood Inn

Robin Hood Farm

1
2
6
7
8

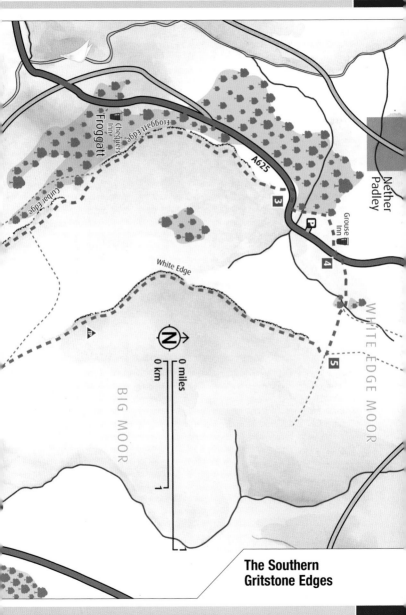

Froggatt

Chequers
Inn

Froggatt Edge

Curbar Edge

A625

Nether
Padley

Grouse
Inn

3

P

4

5

White Edge

WHITE EDGE MOOR

BIG MOOR

N

0 miles

0 km   1

1

**The Southern
Gritstone Edges**

Directions – The Southern Gritstone Edges

➏ Cross the main road at the pelican lights and **bear left** up *Eaton Hill*. **Turn right** at *School Lane* and continue uphill along a road, then track, to *Wellington's Monument*

2 **Retrace your steps** for a short distance then **bear right** and follow the broad path – or a narrower footpath along the top of *Baslow Edge* – to the road at *Curbar Gap*. Cross the road, go through a gate and keep **straight on** along a broad path above *Curbar Edge*. The path continues above *Froggatt Edge*, eventually emerging at a main road.

3 **Turn right** and, in a short distance, go through a hand-gate on the left. Descend to cross a stream and go up to *Haywood* car park. Keep **straight on** across and past the car park to reach a stile in the wall on the right. Cross it and continue across fields to rejoin the main road, just below the *Grouse Inn*.

4 Pass the inn, then cross the road to a gate. Follow the path up to a path junction. **Bear right** and follow the path with a wall on the right to a path crossroads.

5 **Turn right**. Follow the path along the top of *White Edge* for 3km. Shortly after the path begins to descend, the more well-used path descends steeply to the right. *Instead*, keep **straight on** along the less well-defined path to emerge near a road junction.

PHOTO: ANDY HEADING

6 **Turn left,** continue to a road junction, then cross the main road and the stile on the right. **Bear right** to follow the path that runs more or less parallel to the road. Keep **straight on** through a handgate and continue in the same direction into the woodland above the crags of *Gardom's Edge*. Instead of following the often muddy and tortuous path by the wall on the left, make for the top of the crags, where the going is much easier and more pleasant with great views of the *Derwent Valley* below. Eventually you are forced back to the wall on the left, which leads down to a gateway. Once through this follow one of several options in the same general direction past *Moorside Rocks* and down to the main road.

7 Cross the main road to a stile almost opposite, then descend stone steps, cross a footbridge, and continue up to a track. **OR** See **Optional Route** below. Cross this, continue over a ladder stile and follow the concessionary path along the top of *Chatsworth Edge*. *A rail protects a short exposed section.* The path descends a little after the crags peter out, crossing a stile on the right, then climbs again to resume its former course.

8 After crossing a high stone stile, **turn right** and descend through *Chatsworth Park*, **bearing half left** away from the boundary wall on the right, initially using an old grassed-over quarry track. There are stiles across a wooden fence at regular intervals, to permit access to the tarmac drive. Cross this, aim for the left edge of a wood, and continue to a junction with a prominent footpath. **Turn right**, pass through a turnstile then continue into **Baslow**.

▶▶ OptionalRoute ▶▶

The path along the top of *Chatsworth Edge* is exposed over a short section. This can be avoided by **turning right** along the track to walk under the crags and enter *Chatsworth Park* at a lower level. Should this option be taken, on entering the Park continue in the same general direction as the track just used.

STANTON MOOR & ROBIN HOOD'S STRIDE
HILLS, TORS & EDGES

DISTANCE: 15KM/9.4 MILES	**TOTAL ASCENT:** 340 METRES/1100 FEET
START: GRID REFERENCE 247 606	**TIME:** ALLOW 5 HOURS
MAP OS: *OS EXPLORER* OL24, WHITE PEAK, 1:25000	**REFRESHMENTS:** RED LION AND DRUID INN AT BIRCHOVER. DUKE OF YORK AND A CAFÉ AT ELTON. MINER'S STANDARD AND OLD BOWLING GREEN AT WINSTER.
NAVIGATION: STRAIGHTFORWARD.	

ROBIN HOOD'S STRIDE **PHOTO:** *ANDY HEADING*

Stanton Moor and Robin Hood's Stride

15km/9.4 miles

This route combines wild, unspoilt woodland, open moor full of archaeological relics, a gritstone tor, a hermit's cave, and three lovely villages.

Winster – Cowley Knowl – Stanton Moor – Birchover – Robin Hood's Stride – Elton – Winster

Start

Winster. Park in the car park at the eastern end of the village. Grid Reference 247 606

The Walk

The village of **Winster** was established in ancient times. The Domesday Survey, commissioned by William the Conqueror in 1085, lists 'Winsterne', as a village of twenty dwellings. Although the architecture is of interest generally, it is the 16th Century Market Hall that is the real gem. The village expanded in the 18th Century as a result of the lead mining industry.

Not far into our walk, the ruin of an engine house at *Cowley Knowl* testifies to the area's industrial heritage. The section from *Winster* to *Birchover* follows paths through a stretch of unspoilt woodland, before climbing to **Stanton Moor**.

Here we see a total contrast in vegetation – now mainly open heather moor with a scant covering of birch. The moor is littered with excavated Bronze Age burial mounds and we visit the stone circle known as *Nine Ladies*.

After circumnavigating the moor, our descent takes in the old quarry village of *Birchover*. We continue from here along a combination of tracks and field paths on the approach to the gritstone tor of **Robin Hood's Stride**. *Cratcliffe Tor* can be found nearby. At its foot, we find the *Hermit's Cave*, notable for the 12th Century crucifix carved into the rock.

More field paths, a stroll down a quiet lane, then a short, sharp climb, lead us to *Elton*, an attractive village of stone cottages. We finish off by following the *Limestone Way* back to **Winster**.

STANTON MOOR GRAFFITI **PHOTO:** ANDY HEADING

THE TOWER **PHOTO:** ANDY HEADING

PHOTO: ANDY HEADING

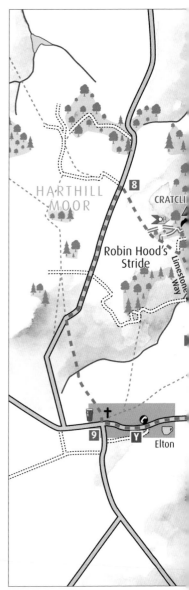
HARTHILL MOOR

Robin Hood's Stride

Limestone Way

CRATCLI

Elton

**Stanton Moor and
Robin Hood's Stride**

Directions – Stanton Moor and Robin Hood's Stride

⑤▸ **Turn right** out of the car park. Walk down the road for 150m and cross the stile on the left. **Bear right** across fields with stiles. At two stile posts (no fence), **bear slightly left** to the bottom corner of the field and a stile hidden from view at first. Continue along the woodland path. On emerging from the wood **bear left** up a track to a gate/barrier.

2 **Turn left** on the path *before* the gate, pass in front of the engine house ruin and then continue on the woodland path. This eventually joins a track. **Turn left** and follow the track for 500m to a fingerpost/stile on the right.

3 Cross this and keep **straight on** up through fields, through *Barn Farm* as waymarked and up to a road.

4 **Turn right** and take the first path on the left. Pass the information board then **fork right** and continue to the stile at *Stanton Moor Edge*. Stay on the left of the fence and continue up to join a higher level path. Follow this around the moor, passing left of the tower folly, to the *Nine Ladies Stone Circle*. Pass the *Circle* on the left then the solitary *King's Stone*, and reach a path crossroads at the corner of a fence.

4 **Turn left** and at the next path crossroads, then **left** again. The path passes right of the triangulation pillar and arrives at the *Cork Stone*. **Turn right** and walk down to the road.

6 **Turn left**. 300m along the road **turn right** opposite the stone factory and follow the descending path to the road opposite the *Druid Inn*. Alternatively, stay on the road to walk through the village to the inn. Cross the road. Take the lane along the left side of the inn. Stay on this, which becomes a gravel track, then follow the old walled track around the hill. At the second gate, again keep **straight on**. After a stile, descend through a field and climb to the main road right of a house. Cross the road and continue on the path to other houses.

7 **Turn right** and go down the lane. Keep **straight on** through a handgate on the left of a gate (*Limestone Way*). Follow the track uphill. Keep **straight on** where this bends right to where the path levels out.* Cross the stile on the left, then that in the wall on the right. Follow the path across two fields to a road.

*  To visit the *Hermit's Cave*, see **Optional Route** below.

8 **Turn left**. Follow the lane for a kilometre to a prominent right-hand bend, then cross the stile on the left (fingerpost on right showing the way). Follow the obvious path through fields first in descent, then uphill to *Elton*. On meeting a lane **bear right**, then **right** again up to *Main Street*.

9 **Turn left**. Walk through the village and continue along the road to a track on the right (*Limestone Way*) opposite *Dudwood Lane*. Follow the track, crossing a lane, and continue uphill to emerge at a road.

10 **Turn left**. Continue across a junction, then follow *Ease Bank* down into **Winster**. **Turn right** to finish.

OptionalRoute

Halfway up this section a stile in the wall to the right of the path gives access to a path to the foot of *Cratcliffe Tor* at the south end of which is the **Hermit's Cave**. To regain the route, retrace your steps for 50m, cross a stone stile adjacent to the wooden one crossed earlier, then **bear half right** aiming for the prominent rocks of **Robin Hood's Stride**.

RUINS OF THE SIGHTING TOWER AND OBSERVATORY ON STANAGE END
PHOTO: BARRY POPE

Bamford Edge & High Neb

16.7km/10.4 miles

A walk with outstanding views, passing over the tranquil heights of Bamford Edge and the more remote northern crags of Stanage Edge.

Hollin Bank – Bole Hill – Bamford Edge – Cutthroat Bridge – Moscar – Stanage Edge – Hollin Bank

Start

Hollin Bank picnic area/car park below Stanage Edge, 3km north of Hathersage. Grid Reference 237 837

The Walk

Footpaths through fields and woodland lead us across the upper reaches of two stunning valleys that descend to join the *Hope Valley* below. Our walk enters the recently designated access land of *Bamford Moor*, following an old overgrown quarry track to **Bamford Edge**. The path runs along the top of the crags that overlook *Ladybower Dam and Reservoir*. The views from hereabouts are breathtaking!

The path beyond the crags narrows for a short distance as it clings to the edge of the slope and takes us through heather and bilberry. After we cross two broken-down walls, the ground levels out. There is a prehistoric hut circle to the right of the path.

A gradual descent around the hillside on a little-used but discernible path leads us to *Cutthroat Bridge*. Two kilometres of ascending footpath and track takes us on to the path that runs the length of *Stanage Edge*. A gradual climb leads past old quarry workings and across the top of the more remote northern crags. Here we reach the highest point on the walk at **High Neb**.

After another three kilometres along *Stanage Edge*, our route ends by descending to the car park along an ancient, paved trail, formerly used by packhorses.

BAMFORD EDGE & HIGH NEB

HILLS, TORS & EDGES

DISTANCE: 16.7KM/10.4 MILES
START: GRID REFERENCE 237 837
MAP OS: *OS EXPLORER*® OL1, DARK PEAK, 1:25000
TOTAL ASCENT: 570 METRES/1870 FEET
TIME: ALLOW 5½–6 HOURS
REFRESHMENTS: NONE ON ROUTE
NAVIGATION: DEMANDS CONCENTRATION FOR A SHORT DISTANCE BEYOND THE CRAGS OF BAMFORD EDGE.

Bamford

Bamford Edge

BAMFORD MOOR

Disused
quarry

4

3

2

Green's
House

North Lees

P

P

5

6

Long Causeway

High
Neb

Stanage Edge

Bamford Edge & High Neb

Directions – Bamford Edge & High Neb

➎ Facing the road, go **left** to the roadside toilets and go through a gate on the far side of the building. Descend the steps then continue downhill through a wood to a stile. **Bear right** across a field, cross a stile in the wall on the right, then resume your former course. The path descends to a stream crossing, after which, take the track **bearing left** up to a stile. Continue across two fields then **turn left** and follow a track towards cottages. Continue along the driveway up to a road.

2 **Turn right**, follow the road uphill to a fingerpost and gate on the left. Pass through and take the grass track uphill a little then **bear left** and contour round. The path continues above and alongside a walled wood, then descends to a fingerpost. Take the **right fork** to *Bamford Road*.

3 **Turn left** at the road and follow it downhill then uphill to the right-hand bend and pass through the handgate on the right.

4 Take the path **forking right**. This climbs gradually to a disused quarry. Use the path that skirts around it on the right then **bear left** above the quarry. The path heads for the edge of the escarpment, with a steep slope down to the left. **Keep to the left** so that you follow the path that runs along the top of *Bamford Edge*. Where the crags end, stay on this narrow footpath as it clings to the top of the steep slope overlooking *Ladybower Dam*. The path runs through heather and bilberry then cuts back into a gully, where you cross a stream.

5 Make for the corner of a high wall straight ahead with a small rock outcrop directly behind it on the uphill side. Continue through the channel thus created and stay with this wall as it **bears right** around the hillside. Where the wall turns to descend to the left at a tiny disused quarry with a solitary pine, follow the path as it **bears right** and downhill to an obvious stream crossing. Go up then **bear left** to join a track. Follow the track down to the A57 at *Cutthroat Bridge*.

6 Cross the road, go through the gate opposite, then follow the path up beside the stream for 50m only. **Bear right** to cross the stream below, then keep **straight on** along the ascending path. Stay on this course, pass *Moscar House* and emerge at a road.

7 Cross over and follow the road opposite for 100m, then **turn right** through a gate. Walk uphill and pass though two more gates. Follow the track downhill, then **bear right** through a gate to keep **straight on** downhill to the *A57*.

8 **Turn right**, then cross the stile on the left. Follow the path uphill to a disused quarry and the first crags of *Stanage Edge*. Take the path that runs along the top of the crags. Pass the triangulation pillar at *High Neb* and continue to a junction with a stony track.

9 Cross this and continue above the rocks for another 150m, then **bear right** downhill along the old packhorse route. The route soon becomes a paved path that leads back to the car park.

BOGGY POOL ON HIGH NEB, STANAGE EDGE   **PHOTO:** BARRY POPE

THREE MOORS

HILLS, TORS & EDGES

DISTANCE: 18.8KM/11.7 MILES

TOTAL ASCENT: 530 METRES/1745 FEET

START: GRID REFERENCE 231 814

TIME: ALLOW 5-5½ HOURS

MAP OS: *OS EXPLORER* OL1, DARK PEAK, 1:25000
OS EXPLORER OL24, WHITE PEAK, 1:25000

REFRESHMENTS: BARREL INN AT BRETTON

NAVIGATION: STRAIGHTFORWARD ON WELL USED FOOTPATHS THROUGHOUT.

PHOTO: *ANDY HEADING*

Three Moors

This walk takes the high ground to the west of Hathersage, offering fine views of the area, and includes open moorland, woodland and riverside.

Hathersage – Leadmill – Eyam Moor – Sir William Hill – Bretton – Hucklow Edge – Abney Grange – Abney Moor – Offerton – Leadmill – Hathersage

Start

Hathersage Pay-and-Display car park. Grid Reference 231 814

The Walk

On leaving **Hathersage**, a path across riverside meadows leads us to a crossing of the *River Derwent*. This is where our climb begins in earnest, first along a lane, then on a footpath up the flanks of *Eyam Moor*. The ascent continues up to the summit of *Sir William Hill*.

Then, the walk takes on a more undulating character, passing a cottage in *Nether Bretton* that sits in an enviable position overlooking *Bretton Clough*, with *Hathersage* and the gritstone tors and edges beyond. When Bonnie Prince Charlie's marauding Jacobite army passed through these parts in 1745, *Bretton Clough* provided local people with a hiding place for their livestock .

A little further on is the *Barrel Inn*, which dates from 1637. A favourite haunt of lead miners through the centuries, it also lay on the 'salt trail' from Cheshire to the Yorkshire towns. Our route continues along a lane that keeps to the crest of *Hucklow Edge*. This offers views to the north of the hills and moors of the gritstone or 'Dark' Peak, and, to the south, of the limestone country known as the 'White' Peak. After passing a gliding club, the route takes a path across open moor, from which there is an unusual, distant, end-on view of *Ladybower*.

Another path leads us across the flanks and over the top of *Offerton Moor*, then descends to 16th Century *Offerton Hall Farm*. A mixture of tracks, field and woodland paths sustains interest en route back to the riverside meadows of the Derwent. The last few metres of our descent are muddy and slippery in wet conditions, making trekking poles a useful accessory.

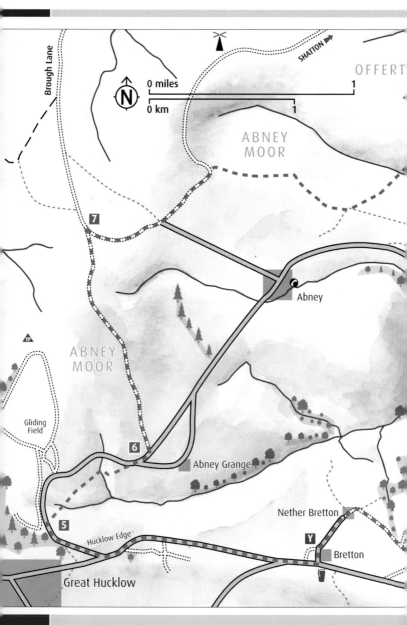

Brough Lane

SHATTON

OFFERT

ABNEY
MOOR

7

ABNEY
MOOR

Abney

Gliding
Field

6

Abney Grange

Nether Bretton

5

Hucklow Edge

Y

Bretton

Great Hucklow

0 miles 1
0 km 1

Three Moors

Directions – Three Moors

⑤► With your back to the car park, **turn right** and walk down to the junction. **Turn left**, then cross the road and take the first **right**. Follow the lane under the railway and on to a gate/stile on the left. Cross this and follow the obvious path to emerge at the main road.

2 **Turn right** and cross the bridge. Continue along the pavement and take the second road on the **right**. Follow this uphill, or take the parallel path on the left of the hedge. Continue past *Hazelford Hall*. The road zigzags then the angle eases as it approaches cottages at *Leam*. Continue to the stile on the right.

3 Cross the stile and **bear left** uphill. Follow the path up the moorside to emerge at a road in about 1.5km. **Turn right** and follow the track up and over *Sir William Hill*, passing the prominent mast, to its junction with a road.

4 Go **straight on**, but take the track on the right. Follow this around past *Nether Bretton* and up into *Bretton*. **Turn right** and continue along the road, then take a **right fork**. Follow the road along the ridge. After a short descent, take a **right fork**. The road climbs and bends to the right then levels out adjacent to the *gliding club* landing strip.

5 Go through the handgate on the right and follow the field path as it descends, then crosses a wet gully just right of a building. The path crosses a stile then **bears right** across more fields, before descending to cross another gully. Keep the same course and emerge at the road further on, having cut the corner.

6 **Turn right**, then cross the stile on the left, which has a bench on the other side. Follow the path across the moor for 1.5km to a junction with a track.

7 **Turn right**. Follow the track as far as the sharp left-hand bend, then keep **straight on** before **bearing right** to follow the path that skirts the hillside to the right. This contours above a wall at first, then descends a little. Where the wall heads downhill to the right, keep **straight on** and reach a footpath crossroads. **Turn left** here. Follow the path over the moor then downhill to the lane adjacent to *Offerton Hall Farm*. (The exit stile is down to the left).

8 **Turn right** and continue along the lane for 400m, then cross a stile on the left. **Bear right**. The path eventually emerges at *Callow Farm*. **Turn left** and cross the stile to the left of the cottage facing. Continue downhill and through a wood to emerge at a track.

9 **Turn right** and continue up the track, then cross a stile on the left in 200m. Follow the descending path to the riverside, the last few metres requiring care in wet conditions. **Turn right** and continue to *Leadmill Bridge*. **Turn left**, cross the bridge, then **turn left** at the stile and retrace your steps to **Hathersage**.

SAM DONOVAN AND KELLY SKIADA **PHOTO:** *ANDY HEADING*

DANE VALLEY & THE ROACHES

HILLS, TORS & EDGES

DISTANCE: 19.5KM/12 MILES	**TOTAL ASCENT:** 570 METRES/1870 FEET
START: GRID REFERENCE 998 662	**TIME:** ALLOW 6 HOURS
MAP OS: *OS EXPLORER* OL24, WHITE PEAK, 1:25000	**REFRESHMENTS:** NONE ON ROUTE

NAVIGATION: MOSTLY WELL MARKED PATHS BUT SHORT SECTIONS ON LESS WELL USED PATHS REQUIRE CLOSE ATTENTION TO THE ROUTE DESCRIPTION.

RAMSHAW ROCKS **PHOTO:** *JON BARTON*

Dane Valley & the Roaches

19.5km/12 miles

A tough but exhilarating outing, taking in a wooded river gorge, the ridgelike crest of a gritstone escarpment, a nature reserve and heather-clad moorland.

Gradbach – Danebridge – Hangingstone – Roach End – Naychurch – Ramshaw Rocks – Gib Tor – Gradbach

Start

Gradbach, riverside car park and picnic area, 4.5km west of the A53 midway between Buxton and Leek, and 3km east of the A54, Buxton to Congleton road. Follow the road for the Youth Hostel.
Grid Reference 998 662

The Walk

From the remote setting of **Gradbach** in the **Dane Valley**, we follow a winding woodland path above the river as it descends through a gorge. Indigenous trees such as oak, birch and ash, and the bilberry beneath them, present a wild countenance.

On arriving at the hamlet of *Danebridge* the climbing starts, and soon our route joins the crest of the long escarpment that forms the gritstone crags of **The Roaches**.

It weaves its way amongst the weathered rocks above the crags. The highest point on the walk offers us extensive views of the Staffordshire countryside. The route then descends to a break in the escarpment, beyond which lie the soaring crags of *Hen Cloud*.

Some interesting route-finding follows, where the right of way is not always obvious, but the stiles are all in place. Soon the path begins the climb along the ridge of *Ramshaw Rocks*, whose jutting, jagged, overhanging rocks serve as a distinctive landmark. Further on, after a short descent through heather, the rocky escarpment leads into *Black Brook Nature Reserve*. Rare bog plants native to this area thrive in its wet climate. From here, lanes, old tracks and field paths lead us through the welcoming final descent.

RAMSHAW ROCKS PHOTO: ANDY HEADING

PAUL MELLOR ENJOYING THE SUNSHINE PHOTO: ANDY HEADING

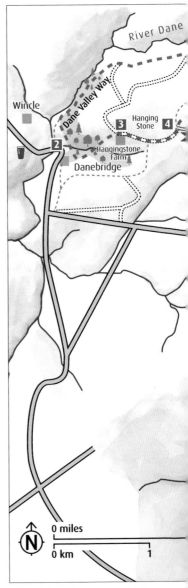

Gradbach

DANE
VALLEY

▲ GRADBACH
HILL

Roach
End

The Roaches

Doxey Pool

5

Black Brook
Nature Reserve

11

Cottage

10

Ramshaw Rocks

9

BUXTON

A53

Well Farm

6

Roch
Hall

Hen
Cloud

8

7

LEEK

**Dane Valley
& the Roaches**

Directions – Dane Valley & the Roaches

↪ **Turn right** out of the car park, follow the road for 200m, then **bear right** down the drive to the youth hostel. **Pass right** of the hostel. Follow the path, then a track as far as a left-hand bend. Keep **straight on** here, cross a footbridge and continue above the river towards *Danebridge*. The path climbs away from the river to pass round the back of two dwellings.

2 About 50m before reaching the bridge at *Danebridge*, **turn left** at the finger post/stile for *Hangingstone*. Climb steps and follow the waymarked path through a wood, then **bear left** up a field to a track.

3 **Turn right**, follow the track above *Hangingstone Farm* and below the *Hanging Stones* to a turning area. **Bear left** up an old track to a fingerpost for *Gradbach*. Continue to a gateway.

4 **Turn left** and ascend the *Gradbach* path to the ridge, then **turn right** to follow the path along this to *Roach End*. Alternatively, you can keep **straight on** to *Roach End*. Cross the road and climb the paved path to the triangulation point on **The Roaches**. Keep **straight on** along the crest for 1.5km to a path crossroads.

5 **Bear left** and descend gradually to a wall that cuts across at right angles. Instead of going through the handgate facing you, walk **left** alongside the wall to another gate. **Turn right** through this then **bear half left**. Pass through two more handgates, then skirt farm buildings to a fingerpost/handgate **on the left**.

6 **Turn right**, follow the track downhill as far as a right-hand bend and gateway.

7 **Bear left** here and walk with a wall on the right, ignoring a stile in that wall, to a stile and stream. Cross these and go up the walled track that has become part of a garden. **Turn right** to walk alongside the wall. Continue to a stile, then **bear left** through the farm and up to the road. **Bear right** to the main road.

8 **Turn left** at the fingerpost to follow the path up through heather to a road. **Turn left** and follow the road to a fingerpost on the right. **Turn right** and follow the path up

and along the crest of *Ramshaw Rocks*. (Easier, less exposed options to the left.) Keep **straight on** past the sign *'Ramshaw Ridge'* to a path junction by a wall.

9 **Turn right**, follow the path for 200m to a fork. **Bear left** with the fence on your right. On reaching a stile on the right, **turn left** to follow the path that descends obliquely through heather. Continue across a stile, keep **straight on** to another on the left, then take the best line across the boggy field to a stile opposite a cottage.

10 Cross the road, **pass right** of the cottage and follow the path beside more rocks. Enter a nature reserve, then keep a straight course until a fingerpost is reached. Walk **right** as directed, skirting the boggy ground, Continue through a wood to a road.

11 **Turn left**, follow the road up and round to the left, then downhill. Keep **straight on** at road junctions then go up the walled track. This ends at a handgate. Keep **straight on** staying close to the wall on the left. Cross to the other side of this when the going is easier on the far side. Continue downhill, pass piles of all sorts and descend to a gate and track. **Bear right**. Stay on this track as it becomes a tarmac lane leading back to the car park.

PHOTO: *ANDY HEADING*

AROUND THE HILLS OF HAYFIELD

HILLS, TORS & EDGES

DISTANCE: 13.5KM/8¼ MILES

TOTAL ASCENT: 640 METRES/2110 FEET

START: GRID REFERENCE 048 869

TIME: ALLOW 5 HOURS

MAP OS: OS EXPLORER OL1, DARK PEAK, 1:25000

REFRESHMENTS: LANTERN PIKE INN AT
LITTLE HAYFIELD

NAVIGATION: STRAIGHTFORWARD

PHOTO: SIMON RICHARDSON

Around the Hills of Hayfield

13.5km/8.4 miles

Stunning views and several hill climbs on bridlepaths characterise this walk amongst the hilly terrain around Hayfield Village.

Bowden Bridge – Peep O Day – Chinley Churn – Lantern Pike – White Brow – Bowden Bridge

Start
Bowden Bridge Pay and Display car park on Kinder Road, a kilometre east of Hayfield village.
Grid Reference 048 869

The Walk
From **Bowden Bridge** where the *Rivers Kinder* and *Sett* meet, a bridleway leads us up steeply to a col on the flanks of *Mount Famine*. The views, both on the climb and from the col, are quite breathtaking.

The route resumes, climbing along a track that brings us to the top of the broad ridge of *Chinley Churn*, with its discarded quarry workings and abandoned stone walls. From here, a two kilometre descent, from which there are distant views of *Kinder Reservoir*, leads us to *Birch Vale*. The route crosses *Sett Valley Trail*, then starts to climb once more along the *Pennine Bridleway*.

We follow the bridleway up to *Lantern Pike*. A diversion along a footpath takes us to the summit, which affords panoramic views of *Black Hill* to the north, *Kinder Scout* to the east, *Mount Famine* and *South Head* to the south and the *Cheshire Plain* to the west.

The descent leads us to *Little Hayfield*, then the last climb takes us up the outlying flanks of *Kinder Scout*. We follow a narrow path through rhododendrons, bilberry and heather, before joining another bridlepath. A stunning view suddenly presents itself on *White Brow* overlooking *Kinder Reservoir*, a man-made phenomenon that enhances the magnificent natural amphitheatre of *Kinder's* steep western flanks.

The descent follows the bridleway and a quiet lane back to *Bowden Bridge* to end the walk.

PHOTO: ANDY HEADING

PHOTO: ANDY HEADING

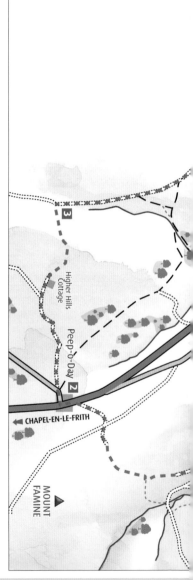

LANTERN PIKE

Birch Vale

River Sett

Sett Valley Trail

A6015

P

LANTERN PIKE

5

GLOSSOP

Lantern Pike Inn

Little Hayfield

4

6

A624

Hayfield

Park Hall

P

N

0 miles

0 km

MIDDLE MOOR

S

P

7

FB
Shooting
Cabin

1

White Brow

Kinder Reservoir

**Around the
Hills of Hayfield**

Directions – Around the Hills of Hayfield

➎ Cross the bridge opposite the car park and follow the road left. This bends right, then further on crosses a bridge and climbs. Take the *'Horses and Cycles'* route via the gate/stile ahead. Follow the bridleway where it leaves the lane and continue up steeply. After a gate, the path levels out. Cross a broad track and follow another track down to the main road.

2 **Turn left**, then cross to the lane leading right. Follow this past *Peep O Day Farm* and keep **straight on** at the bend through a gate. Stay on the track all the way up the hill to *Higher Hills Cottage*. Follow its continuation to the gate on the crest of the hillside. Continue now on the level to a track junction and gate.

3 **Turn right** and keep **straight on** along this as it descends, ignoring all other possibilities. Eventually, the main road in *Birch Vale* is joined. Cross it to a fingerpost and follow the path down to and across the *Sett Valley Trail*. Continue past an angling pond, cross a footbridge, then **bear slightly right** up to a handgate. Follow the obvious path up to a lane.

4 **Turn left**, follow the lane as it zigzags uphill to a road. Cross this and take the steep lane/bridleway just right of cottages. Continue uphill, past a cottage, and through a gate ahead. Leave the bridleway here and ascend steeply by a wall, then **bear right** to the summit of *Lantern Pike*. Continue down the other side to rejoin the bridleway just before a gate. Pass through this. The path **bears right** then bends to the left to cross the large field to a fingerpost and bridle gate.

5 **Turn right** *before* the gate and walk with a wall on the left. The path is vague at first. Continue downhill. On reaching a cottage, cross the drive to a stile and continue the descent, **bearing left** at first. Pass behind the mill conversion and reach a lane. **Turn left** and climb to the main road. (*Lantern Pike Inn* to the left.)

6 Cross the road and follow the unmade road beside *Park Hall Woods*. After the left-hand bend, go through the gate on the right to access *Middle Moor*. Follow the narrow footpath straight up the hillside. On joining a bridleway in 500m, **turn left** and follow this to a path junction below a shooting cabin.

7 **Bear right**, then **right again** in 50m to descend the bridleway. Keep **straight on** downhill, pass through a gateway and join a path running alongside the reservoir boundary wall. **Turn right**, follow it to the reservoir access road, now a concession route, and follow this and the public road back to **Bowden Bridge**.*

*  For an alternate finish, see **Optional Route** below.

Alternatively, cross in front of the gate to the reservoir, follow the path across a foot-bridge, **turn right** to walk alongside the river, then join the road further on.

PHOTO: ANDY HEADING

LOOKING OUT OF THOR'S CAVE **PHOTO:** *ANDY HEADING*

SECTION 3

Limestone Country

Walks in this category are located in the central and southern Peak District. They take in spectacular crag-lined limestone gorges with caves, rock pinnacles and scree slopes rich in fossils. They climb to the tops of prominent peaks, once submarine reef knolls in a tropical sea. They cross limestone upland with fascinating relics of past mining industry. And they often pass through quaint villages with Norman churches, old stone cottages and an inviting inn.

www.scarpa.co.uk

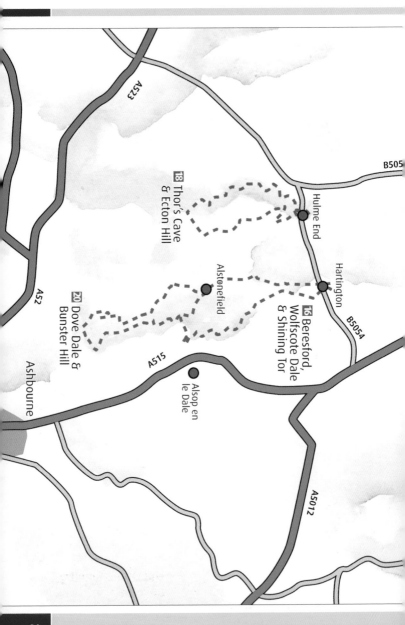

18 Thor's Cave & Ecton Hill

20 Dove Dale & Bunster Hill

16 Beresford, Wolfscote Dale & Shining Tor

Alstonefield

Alsop en le Dale

Hulme End

Hartington

Ashbourne

A523

B505

B5054

A52

A515

A5012

**Limestone Country
Area Map**

TADDINGTON MOOR & CHEE DALE

LIMESTONE COUNTRY

DISTANCE: 15.7KM/9.8 MILES

TOTAL ASCENT: 470 METRES/1540 FEET

START: GRID REFERENCE 149 723

TIME: ALLOW 4-6 HOURS

MAP OS: OS EXPLORER OL24, WHITE PEAK AREA

REFRESHMENTS: CHURCH HOUSE INN AT CHELMORTON

NAVIGATION: STRAIGHTFORWARD

MONSAL HEAD VIADUCT PHOTO: ANDY HEADING

Taddington Moor & Chee Dale

15.7km/9.8 miles

An adventurous excursion that combines rolling limestone upland with an impressive deep river gorge.

Millers Dale – Priestcliffe – Taddington Moor – Chelmorton – Horseshoe Dale – Deep Dale – Wye Dale – Chee Dale – Millers Dale

Start

Millers Dale. Pay-and-Display car park at the former railway station, just off the B6049, 3km south of Tideswell. Grid Reference 138 733

The Walk

We start with a short but steep ascent out of **Millers Dale**. This leads us to easier ground, where field paths and country lanes invite us across rolling upland pastures. A further gradual ascent leads us up on to **Taddington Moor**. This section offers extensive views of the northern *White Peak* and the high *Dark Peak* moors beyond.

Our route then begins a long descent, soon passing through the upland village of *Chelmorton*. Old walled tracks lead us on into the delightful *Horseshoe Dale* and the secluded gorge of *Deep Dale*. Here we find *Thurst House Cave*, whose gaping entrance is a good vantage point for surveying the gorge. The path through *Deep Dale* is awkward in places but we can avoid most of the difficulties by taking a higher level footpath across scree slopes.

As we enter **Chee Dale**, we follow the *Monsal Trail*, the trackbed of a former railway, below some of the most imposing limestone cliffs in the region. We leave the *Monsal Trail* in favour of the narrow riverside footpath that leads downstream through the main part of the gorge.

Stepping stones allow you to cross and continue where the cliffs abut against the river. These can be impassable during or immediately after wet weather, but there is an alternative route to bypass the problem. Beyond the stepping stones the footpath demands care and concentration for some distance as it climbs above the river, before the going gets easy again.

It would be a good idea to take a trekking pole on this walk.

MONSAL TRAIL
AND CHEE DALE
PHOTO: JON BARTON

JON, THOMAS AND WILBUR CROSSING THE WYE PHOTO: GRAINNE COAKLEY

PHOTO: ANDY HEADING

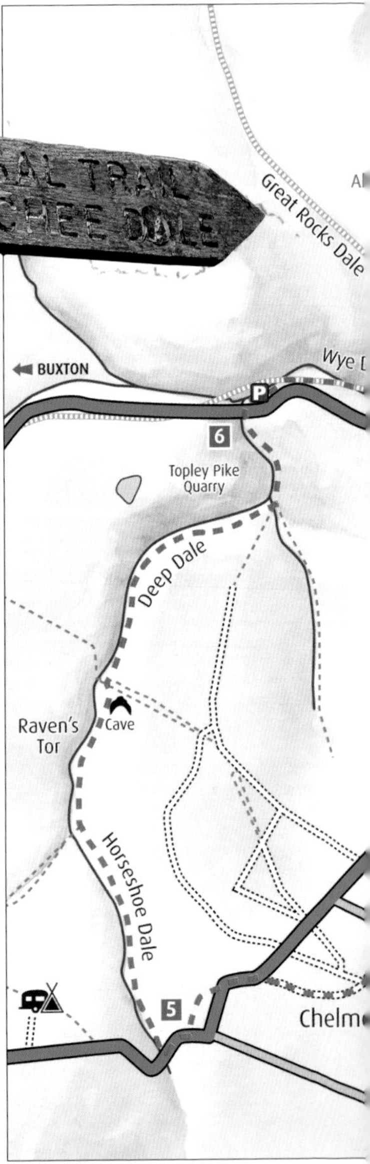
Great Rocks Dale
BUXTON
Wye D
P
6
Topley Pike
Quarry
Deep Dale
Raven's
Tor
Cave
Horseshoe Dale
5
Chelm

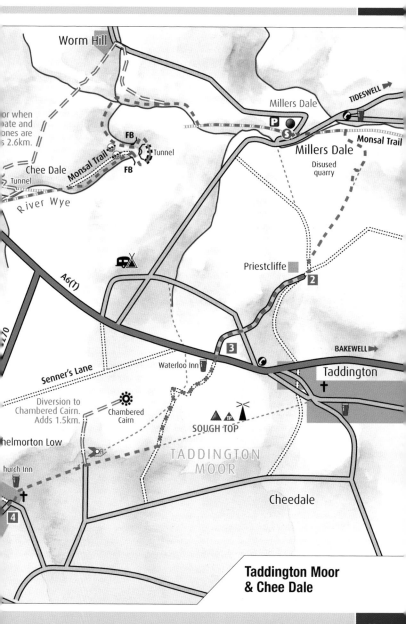

Worm Hill

Millers Dale

TIDESWELL

or when
ate and
ones are
s 2.6km.

P

S

Monsal Trail

FB

Chee Dale

Tunnel

Monsal Trail

FB

Millers Dale

Disused
quarry

Tunnel

River Wye

A6(T)

Priestcliffe

2

Senner's Lane

Waterloo Inn

3

BAKEWELL ▶

Taddington

Diversion to
Chambered Cairn.
Adds 1.5km.

Chambered
Cairn

SOUGH TOP

helmorton Low

hurch Inn

TADDINGTON
MOOR

Cheedale

4

**Taddington Moor
& Chee Dale**

Directions – Taddington Moor & Chee Dale

➊ From **Millers Dale Station**, **turn left** along the *Monsal Trail*, cross the viaduct, then **turn right** to enter a nature reserve (signposted). Continue up steeply beside a disused quarry, then follow a path across fields. On joining a track **turn left** and emerge at a bend in the road in *Priestcliffe*.

➋ **Bear right** and follow the lane. Keep **straight on** at a crossroads to join the A6 opposite the *Waterloo Inn*.

➌ Cross the road and take the track on the left of the inn. Follow this uphill past the zig-zags and continue to where the ground levels out. Pass through a gate. Where there are stiles opposite each other, **turn right**. Continue on the field footpath, cross another track and keep **straight on** down into *Chelmorton*.

➍ Walk past the *Church Inn*, and keep **straight on** along the village street. After passing *Common Lane* on the right, **turn right** at the footpath sign. Follow the drive and keep **straight on** through a backyard gate, over a stile, then through fields to a walled track. **Turn left**. Cross a stile straight ahead where the track turns right. **Bear right** to join another track and follow this to a main road. **Bear left**. Where the road bends left, cross a stile straight ahead, then **bear half left**. Cross another stile and keep **straight on** to join the road further on.

➎ **Turn right**, follow the road downhill, then **turn right** to enter *Horseshoe Dale* by a gate next to farm buildings. Follow the dale downhill, then its continuation as *Deep Dale*. Take the higher footpath option across scree slopes. This avoids all but a short section of potential difficulties underfoot. Exit *Deep Dale* at *Topley Pike Quarry*.

➏ Cross the A6 into *Wye Dale* car park. Follow the riverside track downstream. Cross the river at *Blackwell Mill Cottages*, then continue along the riverside path. Or even better, ascend to the *Monsal Trail* (signposted). Follow this below towering cliffs to the second exit on the left, then descend to the riverside footpath. Continue downstream, footbridges and stepping stones enabling further progress where the cliffs

abut the river. *If the river is in flood and the stepping stones are impassable,*  *see* **Optional Route** *below.* Continue to the end of **Chee Dale**, then double back up to the left to **Millers Dale Station** (signposted).

OptionalRoute

If the stepping stones are impassable, ascend to the *Monsal Trail* between the footbridges. Follow it through tunnels back as far as the second '**Chee Dale**' exit on the right. Descend and cross the river by a footbridge, then go upstream to join another path after a stile. **Turn right** and follow the zigzag path up to a farm. **Turn right**, pass through the farm, continue along the farm track for 500m, then **bear right** on a footpath that is followed via *Flag Dale* to *Wormhill*. **Turn right** at the road, then immediately **right** again to take the descending path into **Chee Dale**. Join the riverside path and as for **6** above.

CHEE DALE **PHOTO:** JON BARTON

LATHKILL DALE & MAGPIE MINE

DISTANCE: 15.8KM/9.8 MILES

TOTAL ASCENT: 370 METRES/1220 FEET

START: GRID REFERENCE 203 664

TIME: ALLOW 5 HOURS

MAP OS: *OS EXPLORER* OL24, WHITE PEAK, 1:25000

REFRESHMENTS: BULLS HEAD PUB AND A CAFÉ AT MONYASH

NAVIGATION: STRAIGHTFORWARD

PHOTO: *ANDY HEADING*

Lathkill Dale & Magpie Mine

15.8km/9.8 miles

The first half is across rolling limestone upland with extensive views, then the character of the walk changes dramatically, as one descends a craggy limestone gorge.

Over Haddon – Magpie Mine – Monyash – Lathkill Dale – Conksbury Bridge – Over Haddon

Start

Over Haddon. Pay-and-Display car park is at the west end of the village. Grid Reference 203 664

The Walk

From the attractive upland village of **Over Haddon**, our route follows field paths across rolling limestone upland with extensive views of the area. The view we get when we arrive at the long-abandoned site of *Magshaw Mine* is stunning! The ground drops away below us into a valley, and rising on the opposite side are parallel lines of white stone walls which draw the eye towards the stark chimney and ruins of **Magpie Mine** at *Sheldon*.

This, our next objective, is fascinating to explore. There is a replica horse gin of the type that was used to raise lead ore to the surface before the installation of a coal-powered Cornish beam engine.

We leave the mine and descend field paths towards *Monyash*. All of a sudden, we are treated to views of the church tower of this former mining village in its sheltered, sleepy hollow. The café and the pub next door provide a choice of refreshment.

Just outside the village, our route enters **Lathkill Dale**. The dale soon narrows and the path becomes rocky, requiring care. The going soon improves as we descend the crag-lined gorge. The stream becomes a river and enters a heavily wooded section with more relics of the lead mining industry. Bateman's House is worth a visit. It lies on the opposite side of the river and is accessible by a footbridge. As the gorge widens, the river passes over several attractive weirs as it heads for the ancient bridge at *Conksbury*. The route now doubles back to provide great views of the gorge as it climbs gradually to **Over Haddon** and the end of our trip.

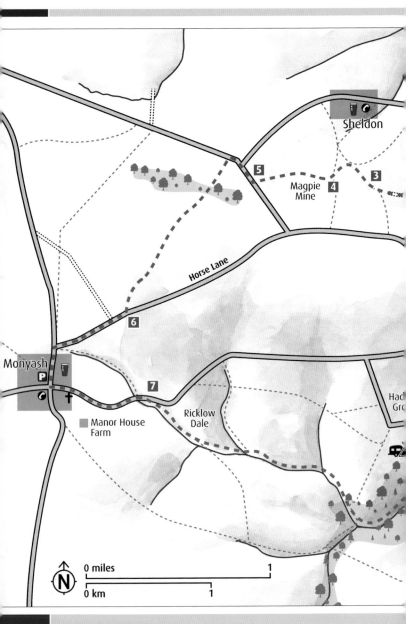

Sheldon

5

Magpie
Mine

4

3

Horse Lane

6

Monyash

7

Ricklow
Dale

Had
Gro

Manor House
Farm

0 miles 1

N

0 km 1

BUXTON ← **A6**

BAKEWELL →

2 Magshaw Mine

...ole Hill Farm

BURTON MOOR

Melbourne Farm

Over Haddon

Y

P

S

Twin Dales

Use this route when shooting is in progress

Lathkill Dale

River Lathkill

8

Conksbury Bridge

Conksbury

Lathkill Dale & Magpie Mine

Directions – Lathkill Dale & Magpie Mine

☛ **Turn left** out of the car park and walk to the junction with *Monyash Road*. **Turn left** and follow the road for 300m to a fingerpost/stile on the right, adjacent to a shed. **Turn right** to follow the obvious path via stiles to a road. Cross this and the stile opposite, then keep going in the same direction across more fields. The path climbs to a high point with evidence of past mine workings in the vicinity.

2 Cross the stile on the right, then another on the left in a few metres to pass through a narrow copse. Continue downhill to a stile by a gate. Cross the road and ascend the old walled track opposite. Continue to a fingerpost.

3 **Bear half right**, cross a stile, then head for a stile in the left corner of the field. Cross this and continue to the ruins of *Magpie Mine*.

4 **Bear right** between the ruins to a stile with fingerpost. Beyond this is another stile, after which **bear slightly left**. Go through an open gateway then **bear right** through another. Now head for the twin wooden pylons, then continue to a stile by a gate to join a road.

5 **Turn right**. Follow the road uphill and past a junction, then cross the stile with fingerpost on the left. Follow the obvious field path through a copse and several fields, finally **bearing half left** to a stile by a gate to arrive at *Horse Lane*.

6 **Turn right** and follow the road downhill to a T-junction. **Turn left** and walk up to the crossroads in *Monyash*. **Turn left** and walk through the village. Follow the road down to the entrance to **Lathkill Dale** on the right.

7 Follow the path down the gorge for over 5km to an assortment of buildings with a road end, a ford and a footbridge – ▶OR▶ see **Optional Route** *below. An escape to Over Haddon can be made at this point by climbing the steep winding lane to the left.* Continue downstream, still on the left bank, for another kilometre to emerge at *Conksbury Bridge.*

8 **Turn left**, continue up to the elbow of the bend in the road, then cross the stile on the left. Follow the footpath along the top of the wooded valley side. In about 400m the path **bears right** uphill away from the rim of the gorge to *Over Haddon*, emerging opposite the *Lathkill Hotel*. Walk past the front of the hotel and keep **straight on** to reach the car park.

OptionalRoute

The concession path is closed on Wednesdays from **October** *to* **January***, which would necessitate the following Optional Route:*
Turn left *where the way is barred and follow the old winding miner's track up out of the gorge to* Mill Farm *and the road.* **Turn right** *and follow the road back to* Over Haddon.

MILL DALE   PHOTO: BARRY POPE

Beresford, Wolfscote Dale & Shining Tor

15.4km/9.6 miles

This walk follows a path alongside the River Dove, through continuously changing gorge scenery, then climbs out to hill country, passing through a handsome upland village.

Hartington – Wolfscote Dale – Shining Tor – Milldale – Alstonefield – Narrowdale – Beresford Dale – Hartington

Start

Hartington, about 19km southeast of Buxton. The walk is described from the market square.
Grid Reference 128 605

The Walk

After a short climb out of the old market village of **Hartington**, our route descends to join the *River Dove* as it enters **Wolfscote Dale**. We follow well-trodden path alongside the winding river, as it flows through the narrow gorge it has etched into the limestone plateau. Occasional crags create picturesque scenes. In parts, the path is hemmed in between steep scree slopes and the river, whilst in others, it traverses wide, flat and inviting grassy areas. After passing through riverside woods **Wolfscote Dale** ends and our route takes to the heights of **Shining Tor** above *Mill Dale*, a short kink in the gorge that forms the link with *Dove Dale*.

Our climb out of the dale is rewarded with views up **Wolfscote Dale**. After a walk in the open, the path descends to cross the little packhorse bridge at *Milldale*. We then climb the lane leading to the fine upland village of *Alstonefield*, with its ancient church, quaint stone cottages and welcoming old inn. Our journey from here uses paths and tracks to make a gradual descent to the *Dove*, once more, where we enter **Beresford Dale**. The riverside path heads upstream through a heavily wooded gorge with a rock spire rising from a pool. It suddenly emerges into the open for the last kilometre back to **Hartington** and the end of our outing.

BERESFORD, WOLFSCOTE DALE & SHINING TOR   LIMITED COUNTRY

DISTANCE: 15.4KM/9.6 MILES

START: GRID REFERENCE 128 605

MAP OS: *OS EXPLORER*® OL24, WHITE PEAK, 1:25000

NAVIGATION: STRAIGHTFORWARD

TOTAL ASCENT: 503 METRES/1652 FEET

TIME: ALLOW 4½–5 HOURS

REFRESHMENTS: GEORGE INN AT ALSTONEFIELD. TEASHOPS AND PUBS IN HARTINGTON.

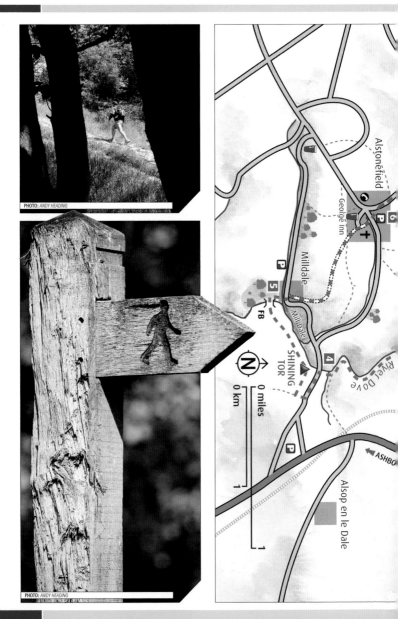

PHOTO: ANDY HEADING

PHOTO: ANDY HEADING

Alstonefield

George Inn

Milldale

Milldale

FB

SHINING TOR

River Dove

N

0 miles

0 km

Alsop en le Dale

ASHBO

NARROWDALE HILL

Narrowdale

8

Wolfscote Dale

3

2

WOLFSCOTE HILL

Devonshire Arms

Hartington

A515

BUXTON →

**Beresford, Wolfscote
Dale & Shining Tor**

Directions – Beresford, Wolfscote Dale & Shining Tor

➊ Facing the *Devonshire Arms*, go left then **turn right** up *Hall Bank*. Take the next road on the **right**, *Reynards Lane*. Follow this uphill for 800m, then **fork right** up a track to rejoin the lane further on.

2 **Turn right**, follow the lane around a left-hand bend, then cross the stile on the right in 100m. **Bear half left** downhill. Continue down an old walled track and across a track junction to reach the riverside footpath.

3 **Turn left**. Follow the path through **Wolfscote Dale** for about 4km to its junction with the road through *Mill Dale*.

4 **Turn left**, then cross the road to a handgate and path leading to **Shining Tor**. Follow this for 300m to the sign for *Pinch Bank*, then **turn right** and ascend steeply as for *Tissington*. A path junction is reached at the top of the steep slope. **Turn right**. Follow the path along the rim of the gorge, then descend the zigzag path to cross the pack-horse bridge at *Milldale* hamlet.

5 **Bear left** at the road, then straightaway **turn right** in front of *Polly's Cottage* and continue up *Millway Lane* for a kilometre to *Alstonefield*. On entering the village keep **straight on** and pass in front of the *George Inn* to reach *Lode Lane*.

6 **Turn left**, then **bear right** to follow the road out of the village towards *Hulme End* and *Hartington*. Continue for 300m beyond the last building to the left-hand bend.

7 Cross the stile with fingerpost on the right, then **bear half left** across fields towards the corner of a small wood. Cross a track and maintain the same general direction across several fields with the ground sloping away to the right. Keep **straight on**, ignoring a stile on the right, and descend to the buildings at *Narrowdale*.

8 **Turn right** along the track, follow it as it bends to the left and for a further kilometre, where it meets a lane. **Turn right** then take the path on the left going upstream alongside the river. Keep **straight on** along this all the way back to **Hartington**.

THE UPPER DOVE VALLEY AND PARKHOUSE HILL **PHOTO:** BARRY POPE

Chrome Hill

13km/8.25 miles

This walk weaves a way through a fascinating area of former reef knolls with distinct peaks, and traverses the fine, narrow limestone ridge of Chrome Hill.

Longnor – Hollinsclough – Fough – Chrome Hill – Dowel Dale – Earl Sterndale – Longnor

Start

Longnor, 13km south of Buxton on the B5053. Park on the square in the village centre.
Grid Reference 088 649

The Walk

From the old market village of **Longnor**, a combination of tracks, field paths and quiet country lanes leads us to the hamlet of *Hollinsclough*, in its sheltered position below the moor. From here we take a bridleway that crosses an ancient packhorse bridge, then gradually ascends a secluded valley. We follow a concessionary path that leads, after a descent and a steep climb, to the start of the ridge of **Chrome Hill**.

Our walk along the ridge is quite exposed in parts, but easier options avoid obstacles if preferred. We soon reach the summit to enjoy the fine panoramic view.

After descending the steep grass slope from the summit, we follow a quiet lane uphill into *Dowel Dale*, past a cave used by Stone Age nomads. A short steep path leads us out of the dale then across to the village of *Earl Sterndale*. Here we can visit the *Quiet Woman*, a quaint old inn whose sign depicts a headless woman!

The last leg of our walk descends to the *Dove Valley* to cross the *River Dove* before a final climb back to **Longnor**.

CHROME HILL   LIMESTONE COUNTRY

DISTANCE: 13KM/8.25 MILES
START: GRID REFERENCE 088 649
MAP OS: *OS EXPLORER®* OL24, WHITE PEAK, 1:25000

NAVIGATION: STRAIGHTFORWARD.

TOTAL ASCENT: 510 METRES/1680 FEET
TIME: ALLOW 4½–5 HOURS
REFRESHMENTS: QUIET WOMAN AT EARL STERNDALE. SEVERAL PUBS AND TEASHOP AT LONGNOR

PHOTO: ANDY HEADING

PHOTO: ANDY HEADING

PHOTO: ANDY HEADING

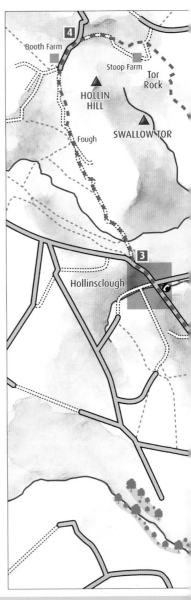

Booth Farm

Stoop Farm

Tor Rock

HOLLIN HILL

SWALLOW TOR

Fough

Hollinsclough

Dowel Dale

6

Dowall Hall

LL

5

Brook

N

0 miles 1

0 km 1

Earl Sterndale

7

8

Green Lane

Beggar's Bridge

River Dove

2

Longnor

S

P

Chrome Hill

Directions – Chrome Hill

➎ From the square, walk past the *Horseshoe Inn* then take *Gauledge Lane*. Follow this to the farm, then cross the squeeze stile on the left opposite the farmhouse. **Bear right** to another stile then keep **straight on**. Ignoring a stile/fingerpost down to the left, keep a straight course to reach a half-hidden stile/fingerpost in the wall on the right, and a road.

2 **Turn left** on the road then take the road on the right to *Hollinsclough*. On reaching the hamlet keep **straight on** past the chapel and up the lane to a bridleway on the right.

3 Follow the bridleway downhill, then across a packhorse bridge. The path climbs steeply to the left to join a track. **Bear left**. Follow the track uphill for a kilometre. Pass over a cattle grid and continue uphill on the lane to a stile on the right next to a gate.

4 Cross this and follow the waymarked route to the left of a fence. Cross a track then follow the waymarked *Concession Path* to **Chrome Hill**. This at first keeps **straight on**, then descends to the right, then climbs steeply to reach the start of the ridge. Follow this direct or use easier alternatives to left or right to gain the summit of **Chrome Hill**. Descend the grass slope keeping to the left. Cross a stile and continue along the ridge or take a lower level path to reach a lane by a cattle grid.

5 **Turn left**, follow the lane up past *Dowall Hall Farm* to a stile on the right 300m further on.

6 Cross this and ascend steeply to a stile. Continue parallel with the wall on the left to a stile on the right of a gate. Cross a track and keep **straight on** down the field with a wall on the right to reach a stile on the right. Cross this and follow the track **left** up to the road or cross the stile on the opposite side of the track and **bear half left** up to a stile. **Turn right** at the road, walk down to a junction and go straight across and up into *Earl Sterndale*.

7 **Turn right** at the *Quiet Woman*. Pass immediately right of the pub and follow the signposted route for *Crowdecote*. The path climbs through two fields then **bears left** after a stile. Follow the descending path, pass through a handgate and head for the private dwelling and a track.

8 **Turn left** and follow the track. Continue past a farm. 50m past a barn on the right, **turn right** at the fingerpost. Cross the wooden stile on the right (not the stone one straight ahead). Keep **straight on**. Cross the *River Dove* at *Beggar's Bridge* and continue across fields and a short boggy area. On reaching a barn, **bear left**. Follow the track uphill. **Turn left** at the top, then take the first road on the **right** and work your way down to the village centre.

CHROME HILL FROM TOR ROCK **PHOTO:** *BARRY POPE*

Thor's Cave & Ecton Hill   13.6km/8.5 miles

A walk through and above the Manifold Valley, visiting an impressive cave in a spectacular situation, and a hilltop with a panoramic view.

Hulme End – Wettonmill – Thor's Cave – Wetton – Ecton Hill – Hulme End

Start

Hulme End. Manifold Way car park on the west edge of the village.
Grid Reference 102 593

The Walk

We set off along the *Manifold Way*, a tarmac track that follows the course of the former *Manifold Valley Light Railway*. Before the tarmac becomes tedious, an interesting track on the opposite side of the river leads to the hamlet at *Wettonmill*.

A further stretch on the *Manifold Way* soon reveals views of our next objective: the giant hole in a limestone cliff, aptly known as **Thor's Cave**. A stiff climb on a paved path leads us to the cave entrance, where we can take in the spectacular surroundings and enjoy an exceptional view up the *Manifold*. This cave yielded several artefacts dating from Romano-British times.

We follow a more gradually ascending path to the upland village of *Wetton*. From here, the nature of the walk changes as our route passes through hilly limestone upland, at first descending then climbing to the summit of **Ecton Hill** for a panoramic view of the area. The rest of our route is all downhill, but it keeps our interest as it passes 18th Century relics and the deep shafts of the *Ecton Copper Mines*.

THOR'S CAVE & ECTON HILL   **LIMESTONE COUNTRY**

DISTANCE: 13.6KM/8.5 MILES

START: GRID REFERENCE 102 593

MAP OS: *OS EXPLORER®* OL24, WHITE PEAK, 1:25000

TOTAL ASCENT: 370 METRES/1220 FEET

TIME: ALLOW 5 HOURS

REFRESHMENTS: ROYAL OAK AT WETTON. NATIONAL TRUST TEASHOP AT WETTONMILL.

NAVIGATION: DEMANDS CONCENTRATION ON THE ASCENT OF ECTON HILL.

PHOTO: ANDY HEADING

[CAPTION] PHOTO: [PHOTOGRAPHER]

[CAPTION] PHOTO: [PHOTOGRAPHER]

Manifold Way

Tunnel

Ecton Bridge

Warslow

B5053

B5054

Manifold Way

ECTON HILL

7

6

FB

FB

FB

8

Westside Mill

Hulme End

P

Thor's Cave & Ecton Hill

Directions – Thor's Cave & Ecton Hill

➊ Follow the *Manifold Way* as far as the road tunnel. **Turn left**, follow the road across the river, then **turn right**. Follow the lane/track to *Wettonmill*.

2 Cross the bridge, then the road, and cross the footbridge by a ford to gain the **old** road down the valley (quieter than the road that follows the old track bed). Where the roads meet, **bear right** along the *Manifold Way* and continue for a further 700m to a footbridge across the river (often dry in summer).

3 Cross it and follow the paved path up to **Thor's Cave**. Continue up immediately left of the cave along a path that leads to a track. **Turn left** and continue to a road.

4 **Bear right**, then **fork left** into *Wetton* village and continue to the first right-hand bend (or **fork right** for public toilets and the *Royal Oak*, then **keep left** to reach the aforementioned bend).

5 **Turn left** (or go **straight on** if approaching from the pub) and **fork left** immediately along a track, then keep **straight on** along a footpath. Pass over a col then descend with a wall on the left. Cross either of two footbridges, then continue uphill along a track/road to a fork in about 500m.

6 **Fork left**, then in 100m **turn right** through a gate. Keep **straight on** uphill along a path, passing old spoil heaps, then other mining relics. The main path passes right of the summit but others lead up left to the triangulation pillar. Continue down the ridge to a former engine house, passing close to several deep shafts.

7 Cross a stile **straight ahead**, then **turn sharp right** to follow the track down to a road. **Turn left** and follow the road down to a T-junction. **Turn right** into *Westside Mill*.

8 **Turn left** as signposted to cross the river by a footbridge, then **bear left** to join the *Manifold Way*. (Often wet to the right). **Turn right** to finish.

LONGSTONE MOOR & CRESSBROOK DALE

LIMESTONE COUNTRY

DISTANCE: 15.8KM/9.8 MILES

START: GRID REFERENCE 185 715

MAP OS: *OS EXPLORER* OL24, WHITE PEAK, 1:25000

TOTAL ASCENT: 465 METRES/1520 FEET

TIME: ALLOW 5 HOURS

REFRESHMENTS: BULL'S HEAD AT FOOLOW, THREE STAG'S HEAD AT WARDLOW MIRES, WEEKENDS ONLY

NAVIGATION: ALL ON ESTABLISHED FOOTPATHS BUT DEMANDS CONCENTRATION ON LONGSTONE MOOR

WATER-CUT, JOLLY DALE. **PHOTO:** JON BARTON

Longstone Moor
& Cressbrook Dale

15.8km/9.8 miles

This route combines a climb to a moorland hilltop, a visit to a quaint old village, and a walk through a limestone gorge.

Monsal Head – Little Longstone – Longstone Moor – Foolow – Wardlow Mires – Cressbrook – Monsal Head

Start

Monsal Head Pay-and-Display car park, just over 1½km northwest of Ashford-in-the-Water on the B6465. Grid Reference 185 715

The Walk

Monsal Head, where our walk starts, is one of the Peak District's most accessible viewpoints. It overlooks the dramatic deep valley of the *River Wye* as it flows through *Monsal Dale* and beneath the arches of the former railway viaduct that spans the gorge.

From here, our route climbs through fields and along old tracks to the cairn at the top of **Longstone Moor**. This is also the site of an ancient tumulus, or burial mound – a commanding location, from which there are distant views of the moors, the gritstone edges and the limestone uplands. Moving on, we gradually descend off the moor and through fields to take us to the village of *Foolow*, with its quaint cottages, its 14th Century market cross and village pond.

Paths that cross wildflower meadows lead us downhill to **Cressbrook Dale**. The *Three Stags Head*, opposite the head of the dale, is always worth a visit. Entering is like stepping back in time, as the interior of the pub echoes its outward appearance.

The path leads straight into the dale and soon passes the prominent limestone rock known as *Peter's Stone*, then climbs the valley side only to descend again. The climb is worth it, however, since the view back up the dale is quite stunning, while in May and June, a fine display of wild flowers makes for a rewarding descent.

Our route continues through woodland and down into *Cressbrook* to enter *Water-cum-Jolly*. The river, here, forms a mill pond before tumbling over an impressive weir. The last leg takes the *Monsal Trail* and crosses the viaduct, then makes the short climb back to **Monsal Head** to finish.

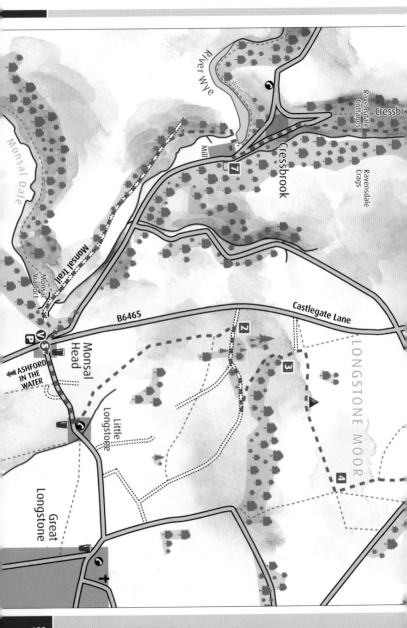

River Wye

Watercum Jolly

Ravensdale Cottages

Cressbr

Cressbrook

Ravensdale Crags

Mill

7

Monsal Dale

Monsal Trail

Monsal Viaduct

B6465

Castlegate Lane

LONGSTONE MOOR

P **V** **S**

Monsal Head

ASHFORD IN THE WATER

Little Longstone

2

3

4

Great Longstone

Longstone Moor & Cressbrook Dale

Directions – Longstone Moor & Cressbrook Dale

➎▶ Cross the main road and follow the pavement to *Little Longstone*. Take the path left by the side of the *Packhorse Inn*, signposted "*Cherpit Lane*". Pass through a handgate, then 50m on the right, another. Continue with the wall on the left and through a third handgate. **Bear slightly right** towards a solitary tree and fingerpost beyond it. Cross a stile and continue uphill on the more obvious path.

2 On emerging at a track, **turn right** and follow this for 500m, then **turn left** into an enclosure with picnic area sign. Cross a stile on the left and continue uphill to a wall with stile.

3 Cross this and **turn right**. Walk uphill parallel with the wall to join an obvious path, then **turn right** and continue up to the cairn. Continue between two copses. The path reaches a path crossroads in 500m at the end of the first of two enclosures on the right.

4 **Turn left**, head for a solitary hawthorn, then **fork left** up to a fingerpost. Continue downhill, cross a stile, then **bear slightly right**. Maintain this direction across fields, crossing a road, a track, another road, then a farm access road. Follow a high wall enclosing a wood round to a stile between gates. Continue across more fields to houses and the main road at *Housley*. Follow the road opposite into *Foolow*.

5 **Turn left** at the junction. Walk to the **left** of the pond and keep **straight ahead** to a half-hidden fingerpost, then follow the alleyway to a gate. **Bear half right** to a handgate, then follow the obvious path through fields. Cross an old walled track and continue in the same direction to join the track further on. **Bear right** and continue to a track junction, then **bear left** to a farmhouse. Leave the track at the bend to cross the stile on the left, then take the **right fork** downhill. Keep a wall on the right, then pass between farm buildings to reach the main road at *Wardlow Mires*.

6 **Turn right**, cross the main road then the *Wardlow Road* and **bear left** to pass in front of *Brookside Farm*. Go through a gate and enter **Cressbrook Dale**. Walk down the dale, pass beneath *Peter's Stone*, then **bear left** up the hillside. (A path runs along the valley bottom through woods but misses the stunning views.) At the top of the valley side **bear right** before a wall to follow the path in descent. The path requires care over a rock step. Continue across a footbridge and stay on the bottom footpath. Pass cottages at *Ravensdale*, follow the lane up to a junction, then descend to a junction at *Cressbrook*.

7 Take the path to the **right**, passing in front of *Cressbrook Mill Apartments*. Where the path meets the pool, **turn left**, cross the footbridge over the torrent below the weir and continue up to the *Monsal Trail*. Follow this to where it ends at a tunnel immediately after crossing the viaduct, then follow the path up to **Monsal Head**.

PETER'S STONE PHOTO: BARRY POPE

DOVE DALE & BUNSTER HILL

LIMESTONE COUNTRY

DISTANCE: 13.5KM/8.5 MILES

TOTAL ASCENT: 560 METRES/1830 FEET

START: GRID REFERENCE 147 508

TIME: ALLOW 5 HOURS

MAP OS: OS EXPLORER OL24, WHITE PEAK 1:250000

REFRESHMENTS: IZAAK WALTON HOTEL NEAR THE START AND FINISH, TEAS AND REFRESHMENTS BUT NO CAFE AT MILLDALE, GEORGE INN AND TEASHOP AT ALSTONEFIELD

NAVIGATION: STRAIGHTFORWARD, ALTHOUGH THERE IS A NEED FOR CONCENTRATION AT ILAM TOPS ABOVE DOVE DALE

PHOTO: SARAH FORD

Dove Dale & Bunster Hill   13.5km/8.5 miles

This walk includes a limestone gorge with spectacular rock features and crags, a particularly attractive upland village, and a hilltop with superb views.

Dove Dale – Milldale – Alstonefield – Stanshope – Hall Dale – Ilam Tops –
Bunster Hill – Dove Dale

Start
Dove Dale car park, situated equidistant from Thorpe and Ilam, northwest of Ashbourne and 4km west of the A515.
Grid Reference 147 508

The Walk
Our walk starts with us following a path upstream into the narrow limestone gorge of **Dove Dale**. The path passes beneath the steep flanks of *Thorpe Cloud*, a former reef knoll that grew from the sea bed in a limey tropical sea over 300 million years ago. Further on we come to the impressive *Tissington Spires*, the natural arch near *Reynard's Cave* and *Lion's Head Rock*. On the other side of the *Dove* is the tower-like *Ilam Rock*.

Six hundred metres further upstream, we come to *Dove Holes*, which were etched out by the river when it flowed as a torrent at a higher level. Eventually, the path crosses an ancient packhorse bridge and enters the hamlet of *Milldale*.

Our route leaves the gorge at this point to climb to *Alstonefield*. This is a delightful upland village of old stone cottages, an Elizabethan Manor House and a 15th Century church. The route loses height from *Alstonefield*, only to climb again, giving us the chance to descend one of **Dove Dale's** tributary dales.

Hall Dale is a dry valley, down which the path drops steeply over a few metres near the confluence. Alas, our route climbs again from here, this time up steps – lots of them – leading up to the top of a steep wooded slope. A narrow path, which requires care, continues across the top of the woods.

Suddenly, the path emerges into the open at *Ilam Tops* to reveal a breathtaking view across the gorge. It crosses high pastures to reach the top of **Bunster Hill** overlooking *Ilam*. After a grassy descent a path leads us across the flanks of the hill back to the start.

Ilam

BUNSTER HILL

Ilamtops Farm

Cottage

7

6

River Dove

Dove Dale

Natural Arch

Izaak Walton Hotel

THORPE CLOUD

8

S

FB

Stanshope

Alstonefield

4

3

P

Hall Dale

P

Millway

2

Milldale

Dove Holes

Mill Dale

A515

**Dove Dale
& Bunster Hill**

Directions – Dove Dale & Bunster Hill

⑤➤ From the car park walk past the toilet block and follow the path upstream on the left of the river. Unless the river is very low, cross the footbridge and continue on the right bank. The path improves in 300m. If the river is low, stay on the left side of the river, then cross at stepping stones. Continue up the gorge on the undulating path for 4km, where the path crosses the river by an old packhorse bridge to enter *Milldale*.

2 **Turn left,** then **first right** and pass in front of *Polly's Cottage* to follow *Millway* uphill to *Alstonefield*. 150m beyond the church **bear left**, then keep **straight on** to a junction.

3 **Turn left**, then take the first track on the **left** (50m). Keep **straight on** along this to where it bends **sharp right**. Leave the track, cross the stile and keep **straight on** with a wall on the right. Cross a stile and **bear right** with the wall to descend steeply to a road. Cross the road and continue up the track opposite. This leads to the hamlet of *Stanshope*.

4 At the junction, **turn left** along a track then in 100m cross the stile on the right. Follow the path across fields, down into *Hall Dale* and so to the *River Dove*.

5 **Turn right** and walk downstream alongside the river to a waymark post in 150m. **Bear right** to follow the stepped footpath up to the top of the woods and the valley side. Continue along the top edge of the wood along a narrow footpath. Eventually the path exits the wood at a stile.

6 **Bear slightly left** downhill as directed by the fingerpost. The path becomes narrow as it skirts below an isolated cottage then **bears right** through two stiles on its far side to emerge on the cottage drive. **Turn left** and follow this as far as the gateway to *Ilamtops Farm*.

7 **Turn left** and walk along the avenue of trees and through a gate. Keep **straight on** here with a wall on the right. Cross a stile in the corner ahead (*Bunster Hill* sign). Keep more or less **straight on** to the top of **Bunster Hill**. Retrace your steps as far as the stile. Instead of crossing it **turn left** and descend with a wall on the right. Ignore a stile on the right in 100m and continue as far as a definite path cross roads with a stile on the right.

8   **Turn left** here to follow the path across the flanks of **Bunster Hill**. Continue through a gap on the ridge then **bear left** downhill. Cross a stile and maintain the same direction across fields to reach the back of the *Izaak Walton Hotel*. **Bear left** to return to the car park.

STEPPING STONES OVER THE RIVER DOVE   **PHOTO:** *BARRY POPE*

For every footpath, hill top and rainy day the Peak District has a corresponding refreshing café, sheltering pub and accommodating B&B. While we have our favourites, there are so many that it is impossible for us to recommend any in particular. Likewise we know and work with many outdoor enthusiasts and businesses – too many to mention all of them. However **Vertebrate Graphics** has a few acquaintances that you might find useful:

Two excellent websites are worth a look for any visitors to the Peak District: **www.peakdistrictonline.co.uk** is a brilliant hub for what to do and see in the area, while its sister site **www.peakdistrict-nationalpark.com** is a good first point of call for accommodation and other visitor information.

Are your boots letting in water? **Feet First**, a local company, is the UK's specialist repairer and resoler of all types of outdoor footwear. Check out their service on **www.feetfirst.resoles.co.uk**.

Our thanks go out to **Scarpa**, **Rab** and **Lowe Alpine** for kitting us out in excellent gear for the production of this book.

There are many excellent outdoor shops dotted around the Peak and surrounding area. Over the years **Foothills** in Sheffield has never failed to give anything less than a first class service to the walking community.

Vertebrate Graphics Ltd is a full-service graphic design, publishing and website producer. We specialise in the outdoor leisure market. Look at our portfolio of work on **www.v-graphics.co.uk** if you are interested in our services.

Vertebrate Graphics

Fill in this coupon and send it along with a cheque to:

Vertebrate Graphics, Crescent House, 228 Psalter Lane, Sheffield S11 8UT

Make cheques payable to Vertebrate Graphics Ltd. Unfortunately we are unable to accept credit card payments. Orders dispatched by return.

MLTUK Handbooks are available from

Mountain Leader Training UK
Siabod Cottage,
Capel Curig,
Conwy LL24 0ET

T: 01690 720 272
E: info@mltuk.org
W: www.mltuk.org

Item	Qty	Price (inc. P&P)
South West Mountain Biking Book		£14.95
South West CD-ROM		£5.95
Dark Peak Mountain Biking Book		£14.95
Dark Peak CD-ROM		£5.95
Peak District Bouldering		£14.95
	TOTAL £	

Name: ....

Address: ....

....

Postcode: ....

E-mail: ....

☐ **Vertebrate Graphics** will never pass on your details to third parties, but if you do not want to receive information on future VG Hill Walking, Mountain Biking or Climbing and Bouldering Guides, please tick here.

STAFFORDSHIRE GRIT
The Roaches

peak district : bouldering
written by Rupert Davies & Jon Barton

finitive climbing guide
routes and boulderin
on Staffordshire gr

Dark Peak
Mountain**Biking**
True Grit Trails

Written by
Paul Evans

South West
Mountain**Biking**
Quantocks · Exmoor · Dartmoor

Written by
Nick Cotton

hillwalking
The official handbook of the **Mountain Leader** and **Walking Group Leader** schemes

rockclimbing
ESSENTIAL SKILLS & TECHNIQUES
The official handbook of the
Mountaineering Instructor and **Single Pitch Award** schemes

books by
Vertebrate Graphics

britain's most **successful** outdoor leisure books

"*peak district bouldering* – a thoroughly **excellent** guidebook: informative, stylish, practical, & inspiring."
Planet Fear

"*dark peak mountain biking*, the peak's **best ever** mountain bike guide."
Singletrack Magazine

"*rock climbing* – it's a **tremendous** achievement to bring together another, such **high quality** volume so soon after *hillwalking*, **well done!**"
Mountaineering Council of Ireland

 Vertebrate Graphics Ltd
Crescent House, 228 Psalter Lane, Sheffield, S11 8UT

0114 267 9277
www.**v-graphics**.co.uk

Woodbine Café

In the heart of the Peak District

B&B

Home cooked food,
especially for walkers, mountain bikers
and other lovers of the Peak District.
Excellent, comfortable accommodation.
Group bookings welcome

18 Castleton Road, Hope, Hope Valley, Derbyshire, S33 6RD
© 07778 113 882